T0062399

L.A. RULES

W.R. Chadbourn

Order this book online at www.trafford.com
or email orders@trafford.com

Most Trafford titles are also available at major online book retailers.

© Copyright 2009 W.R. Chadbourn.
All rights reserved. No part of this publication may be reproduced, stored in a retrieval
system, or transmitted, in any form or by any means, electronic, mechanical, photocopying,
recording, or otherwise, without the written prior permission of the author.

This book is a work of fiction. Names, characters, places and incidents are the product of the
author's imagination or are used fictitiously. Any resemblance to actual events, locales,
or persons, living or dead, is coincidental.

Photo Credit Tigran Tovmasyan

Note for Librarians: A cataloguing record for this book is available from Library
and Archives Canada at www.collectionscanada.ca/amicus/index-e.html

Printed in Victoria, BC, Canada.

ISBN: 978-1-4269-1473-7 (Soft)

*Our mission is to efficiently provide the world's finest, most comprehensive
book publishing service, enabling every author to experience success.
To find out how to publish your book, your way, and have it available
worldwide, visit us online at www.trafford.com*

Trafford rev. 10/01/2009

 www.trafford.com

North America & international
toll-free: 1 888 232 4444 (USA & Canada)
phone: 250 383 6864 ♦ fax: 812 355 4082

The major civilizing force in the world is not religion, it is sex.
Hugh Hefner

TABLE OF CONTENTS

GENESIS

September 7, 1977.

I am sitting in the Harvard Law School cafeteria with a bunch of 2Ls from my study group. It's the first week of class and we are supposed to be studying civil procedure. Instead we are talking about jobs. After all, as the civil procedure professor says, "This is trade school."

"So, did you like your firm this summer, Richard?" asks Ronda.

Ronda is the older, mature type. She sports the suburban mall inspired frizzed out page boy look. Her husband divorced her. Hubby had Ronda represented by his best friend. Ronda got the grand piano and nothing else. She applied to law school the same year Hubby moved out.

"You know," I say. "It isn't the firm. It's Manhattan. It's just too difficult. The city has some kind of monopoly on aggressive behavior."

"You really should try LA," says Sam.

Sam is some blond guy from Minnesota. He could swing to either coast or Chicago for that matter. Low content.

"Man, go to LA," says David.

David is a red haired kid from Beverly Hills flats via University of California at Davis. I couldn't find Davis on a map. He is very impressed with the fact that he is at Harvard. I am not. David is not high content.

"California has the life style," says Sam, Sam.

Sam, Sam got the name because he got called on second on the first day of tort class, after single Sam. Now Sam, Sam is worth listening to. Sam did a nickel for armed robbery at San Quentin. Sam has the Fu Man Chou moustache and the chain gang tan. He also has a high

1

school equivalency degree from prison. Governor Brown had personally pardoned him and here he is at Harvard Law School, from criminal to corporate lawyer. Way more perks than a prison gang. Sam, Sam is not interested in death row appeals. He likes securities law. There is clearly money in rehabilitation.

Fast forward. July 5, 1979.

Another summer job at another law firm in Manhattan. I'm writing a request for a revenue ruling that will probably not be read during the lifetime of my unborn children. The temperature is 96 degrees and the humidity must be 104 percent. I'm sitting in the law firm cafeteria with a couple of other clerks drinking regular coffee and looking out the window at what seems less like rain and more like steam.

"I'm moving to LA," I say to nobody in particular.

"Are you nuts?" Bob from NYU says. "Every street is a super highway."

"He is doing it for sex," says Ellen from Columbia.

Ellen has the same accent as the guys who try to sell you a hot knish on the beach at Coney Island.

"They're all so gorgeous out there that they can't keep their hands off of each other," Ellen says.

I tell my parents a month later. I am standing in front of the refrigerator. It is a beautiful summer evening in Hackensack.

"Richard, Los Angeles is a big nothing," my father says. "They haven't even got a downtown."

I wince.

My father pauses dramatically.

"You are not moving to Los Angeles for sex, are you?" he says. "There is plenty of sex in New York."

HOME COOKIN'

I am looking at Kimberly's green eyes.

Fog is rolling off the top of the Jacuzzi. Behind Kimberly, the lights of Malibu are twinkling and I hear the dull roar of the Pacific Ocean.

It is getting increasingly difficult to focus.

Kimberly's breasts keep shifting in and out of the foam on the surface of the Jacuzzi. I decide that further efforts to think are pointless. A bottle of Cakebread Chardonnay and a doobie have erased any traces of eight years of higher education.

I look meaningfully at Kimberly's eyes and slowly and purposefully pull the thermometer out of the Jacuzzi. The temperature is 107 degrees. No wonder my brain is cooking. My penis probably looks like a Coney Island hot dog.

Wrong move. Kimberly evidences a primordial response to something phallic. She moves closer to me in the Jacuzzi fog. She has a pretty face. Her green eyes are framed by wet, jet-black hair.

Kimberly's hands disappear under the bubbles. A triangular piece of back fabric floats to the surface and then floats off. She straddles me. Her teeth fasten on my ear lobe.

"I want you," she says.

Kimberly's conversational powers suddenly become irrelevant. A single thought starts in my medulla oblongata and soon takes throbbing control of my entire cerebral cortex: *I can't get an erection.*

I mentally start turning the pages of 1950s fetish magazines. The images of big hair, garters and stockings dissolve to a hot dog cooking on turning metal rollers at Nathan's in Coney Island. Kimberly is still rocking back and forth. She is moaning. Her breasts are in my face. They smell vaguely like chlorine.

I can't perform, I think, because I am being cooked. The solution. Get out of this giant Crock-Pot. My father had a partner who regularly said that the two most overrated things in life were home cooking and home fucking. Now, the two vectors have converged.

"Let's go to bed," I say.

I realize that I am not being particularly original, but Kimberly takes the cue.

She smiles and turns. I follow. Her ass is an inspiration.

We walk hand and hand down the hallway over the shag carpet. I open the sliding glass doors and turn down the dimmer switch until the lights barely glow. Kimberly pulls down the bed covers. I caress her. She caresses me. Her tongue starts to dart in and out of my mouth. She spreads her legs. I mount her and we both rock back and forth to a climax.

The bed is empty the next morning. The sunlight is brilliant. I feel elated and dehydrated at the same time. This is my first day in Los Angeles. I have a job lined up as a tax associate at the venerable downtown law firm of Snodgrass & Pecham. I just need to take the California bar exam.

Cary tells me that we are going to cruise and look for an apartment for me. We get in his red GTO and drive south down the Pacific Coast Highway. I make him stop at a Circle K and drink an entire bottle of lime green Gatorade. I am definitely feeling better.   We drive down Santa Monica Boulevard.

"Santa Monica is a possibility," Cary says.

"Who lives here?" I ask.

"Professionals, liberals, Jane Fonda," he says.

"Keep going," I say. We drive a few miles further south.

"We could try Venice," Cary says.

"Who lives here?" I ask.

"Mixed," Cary says. "Artsy. Lots of dopers."

"Keep going," I say. We drive a few miles further south.

"What's this," I ask. There are suddenly blocks and blocks of apartments facing moorings for boats. The streets are even wider than the normal Los Angeles streets. We pull down the main drag. It seems like it is a hundred yards wide.

"This is Marina Del Rey," Cary says.

"Who lives here?" I ask.

"Singles," Cary says. "It's pricey."

"Find the rental office," I say.

Cary pulls over and I get out of the car to try to find a rental office. There is, of course, nobody on the street. Nobody walks in LA. A red Sting Ray convertible with black Nevada plates pulls over with two blonds in matching terry cloth shorts and halter tops. These girls could be on their way to a *Penthouse* photo shoot. I have never seen women look this good without a staple at their waistline.

"Where are all the boats?" says the blond in blue terry cloth.

"You have to go one block west to get to the boats," I say.

"We're supposed to party on a boat," says the blond in the yellow terry cloth.

"Well, good luck," I say. "You girls look like you would be a big plus at any party."

"You're nice," says the yellow terry cloth blond.

I turn to Cary.

"I am definitely living here."

The Sting Ray's engine throbs and blue exhaust fumes shoot out under the black Nevada plates.

I call my mother that night from the hotel and I give her my new address.

"42971 Bora Bora."

"Richard, what kind of address is that?" she says.

"The streets are very long out here, Mother. Everything was developed after the private automobile," I say.

"Oh," she says.

A week later I am at my first firm cocktail party. I am talking to the senior partner who runs the business department at Snodgrass & Pelham. The guy looks like a movie star. Eventually, somebody tells me that he was a movie star. He made a couple of action films in the thirties. Jimmy Cagney was in one of them.

"So, Richard, where have you decided to live?"

"I found an apartment in the Marina, Sir."

"Have you joined the Marina City Club, young man?"

"No, I haven't, Sir."

He gives me a look of confidence.

"You really don't need to," he says. "There is plenty to go around."

HOT WHEELS

The phone rings. It is Saturday morning. I'm in my room at the Biltmore Hotel. My firm has very kindly offered to pick up "transition expenses." My alarm clock says 6:30 am. My elbows itch. Who washed the sheets with caustic chemicals? I have a bad headache.

I pick up the phone.

"What asshole is this?" I ask.

"Rise and shine, Ritchie," says the voice on the other end.

"Why are you torturing me, Stanford?" I ask.

"I am not torturing you," Stanford says. He sounds very empathetic. "I have been working hard on integrating you into Los Angeles society. You're going to have breakfast with my father today and buy a car. Remember the program. You need wheels first, music second, and then, third, a woman."

"Ok, Ok," I say. I'm not that talkative at 6:30 am. This isn't the first time I have heard Stanford's three point plan.

"Be there by 8:30," Stanford says. "I got to have coffee with one of the other grad students. Bye."

I am sure that the grad student is female and born with the assistance of a midwife in a small village somewhere in Eastern Europe. In the shower, I am overwhelmed by the irony of all of this. Here is the crazed Los Angelino I met at the London School of Economics calling me from Boston to tell me that he is advancing my integration into LA society. Actually, having met his father in London, he probably is.

I get in the rented Toyota Celica and get on the 405. I like driving over the 405 to the Valley. The Toyota's engine starts to whine past Westwood as we head up the hill. At the crest the whole valley lies

7

ahead. I pick up speed downhill until I hit the 101 and take the Encino exit. I like the Valley. Life has simple rules and everybody's house is for sale at the right price. The problem is the summer when the valley is just too stinking hot. The Blitstein's live in one of these gigantic split-level houses with palm trees outside. Mr. Blitstein invites me out for breakfast. He is obviously ready for a little *mano a mano* conversation. He drives me to breakfast in his wife's pearl white Mercedes. This Mercedes is so big it doesn't even have a number on the trunk. He drives to some coffee shop on Ventura Boulevard. Not much conversation in the car. I am thinking that the only places I have ever eaten in the Valley are coffee shops. The Valley must be some kind of Mecca for coffee shop owners.

Mr. Blitstein is very fussy about the table. It has to be in the front. It can't be too close to the door. The hostess is looking a little exasperated, but Mr. Blitstein ignores her. Mr. Blitstein is going to find the right table. Finally, we sit.

"Have pancakes, Richard," says Mr. Blitstein. "They are good here."

"I'll have pancakes," I say to the waitress. I notice that she has blond helmet hair. Her morning make up must be responsible for serious Ozone depletion. I am guessing it is a Valley thing.

"Ok, hun," says the waitress.

"I'll have the same. And I want hot coffee," says Mr. Blitstein. "Make sure the coffee is hot."

"OK, hun," says the waitress.

"So," says Mr. Blitstein. He is a man who gets right to the point. He is not the kind of guy I would like to deal with across a conference room table. Mr. Blitstein builds shopping centers. They are sprawling stucco monstrosities. I have a feeling my sentiments are shared by most retailers who have leased any space in his shopping centers.

"Stanford says that you need to buy a car."

"Yes, sir," I say.

"What kind of car?"

"I am thinking of a Chrysler Cordoba. You know the rich feel of Corinthian leather."

"Stop fooling around Richard," says Mr. Blitstein. "Professional people don't drive that car. That is a car for Mexicans. You need something dependable. Something reliable. You need a German car. You are going to buy a Volkswagen."

"OK," I say. "I am going to buy a Volkswagen."

I have already understood that it pointless to argue with Mr. Blitstein. As his son would say, he has very highly defined rules governing the natural order. There appears to be one genus – German car. There appeared to be two species. Mercedes for mature people. Volkswagen for young people. Darwin lives on in Los Angeles.

Just then, Mr. Blitstein gestures at the bus boy.

"*Agua fria.*" I observe that the bus boy looks like he was originally from Bombay.

"I don't think he understands Spanish," I say to Mr. Blitstein.

"*Agua fria,*" repeats Mr. Blitstein.

I am very confident that I have made the right choice in cars.

In the car on the way back to the Blitstein's, I am thinking about this guy Roy Lichtenstein I knew in high school. He wanted a Pontiac. His father wanted to buy him a Beetle. Roy knew his audience. He went to the school library and took out a book with pictures of Adolph Hitler saluting the Volkswagen factory workers from the back of a beetle. I remember that Roy's Pontiac was fire engine red.

"I'll call you on Tuesday, Richard," says Mr. Blitstein.

"Thank you," I say.

The phone rings on Tuesday morning.

"We are picking up the car tomorrow," says Mr. Blitstein. The logistics turned out to be quite elaborate. I have to drop off my rental car in some dead end street behind the airport. Even though the drop off is early, they charge me the same price. Then, I drive with Mr. Blitstein down the 101 to the far reaches of the valley. I see many housing projects under construction. I see pink signs that say, "The Valley is Bank of A. Levy Country." I'm pretty sure I am in a different valley than Mr. Blitstein's Valley.

There is my car. It is a Rabbit. It is cobalt blue metallic, as the salesman says. It has a stick shift. Much better on mileage, according to

Mr. Blitstein. As it turns out, Mr. Blitstein has called every Volkswagen dealer in Los Angeles and quite a few in Nevada. My Rabbit is the cheapest Rabbit sold in all of North America that year.

As I drive back to Los Angeles, I think, "I've got wheels." Part one of the three-part program is completed.

Next weekend I go to Crazy Eddy to solve the music problem. I ignore the unctuous salesman and buy a huge stereo system with a gigantic pre amp with tubes that glow in the dark and three foot high speakers that throb when you turn up the bass. They look good in my apartment facing the couch.

Like the song says, two out of three ain't bad.

REMORSE

I knew it would happen.

Right after the bar exam, one week before I actually am to begin work, I begin to think negative thoughts.

For two days I get up at 6:00 am, drive down to 96th Street, and watch the planes taking off for New York. I think about what it would be like to be on one.

The bar exam is not going to be fun. I do not like having to take an exam to practice a trade. It makes me feel like a plumber or an electrician. Moreover, even coming from the very tip top of my class at Harvard Law School, I really do not know any California law. It is not like the law in New York or Massachusetts. Generations in the sun and constant earthquakes had created the need for California lawyers to write everything down in statutes. As soon as some court decides something, the legislature enacts a statute. The statutes have exceedingly long numbers, like Chapter 16, section 16-9071. In other words, California law is like the street addresses on Bora Bora Avenue.

I am lost. I needed the equivalent of the Thomas Brothers Street Map to California law.

The bar review book seems to do the trick. It is written by another sun crazed Californian. It contains only the basics. They ask this – you say this. You aren't even expected to know all of the long section numbers. You could say the legal equivalent as it is right near the corner of Wilshire and Fairfax. Everybody knew what you meant. The bar review courses are a great help. The lecturers seem like comedians. Somebody explains to me during a coffee break that most of them actually are comedians and a few of them actually have had gigs in clubs on Sunset Boulevard.

On the weekends, there are no bar review courses and I need to study. David from law school suggests that I study at the UCLA law library. I lamely take him up on the suggestion. I soon realize that his suggestion has a darker, ulterior motive. I begin my regime of studying at the UCLA law library. It opens at 8:00 am. I arrive having drunk a large cup of take-out coffee from the Circle K. I sit in a nice sunny spot and piece by piece commit the basics of community property law to memory. A walk outside and a Circle K sandwich for lunch. Back to my sunny spot.

However, around 3:00 in the afternoon I start hearing distracting noises.

On the second Saturday, I close my book in the middle of a particularly difficult section dealing with couples that get married in separate property states and then have the good fortune to move to California where the wife's lawyer seems to get all the property. I survey my environment. It has changed. Ten feet in front of me I see an eighteen-year-old pear shaped ass in track shorts, framed at the top with platinum blond hair, bending over to pick up a purse. The activity is being observed approvingly by a table of eighteen-year-old blonds of various shades of sub-platinum who are all wearing lots of mascara and blue eyeliner. I inspect the platinum hair framed ass, which seems to be stationary for a long time. I then glance at a table full of eighteen year old blonds and am met with a row of smiles showing off exceedingly white teeth.

I am embarrassed. Here are all of these adolescent chicks watching me check out this other chick's ass and seemingly approving of it. The face attached to the pear shaped ass then turns and flashes a gleaming smile. That is it. I decide I could still fail the community property questions and pass the bar exam. I leave the law library and drive home.

I am overcome with lust. I masturbate wildly, fanaticizing about the sex triathlon where the gold, silver, and bronze medalist all model their rear ends with their medals as sort of reverse belt buckles with their track shorts down around their ankles. The national anthem is blaring on the loud speaker while I climax.

Very shortly thereafter I get a call from Blitstein. I describe what has transpired, other than the self-gratification part.

"It's a set up," he says.

"What do you mean?"

"Where do you think the UCLA undergraduates hang out when they want to date a lawyer? *In the law library*. Are you a moron?"

I am very quiet. I am digesting this morsel. I ask how Blitstein's Romanian girlfriend is doing. I don't really care and sort of tune out the response.

I start thinking. That son of a bitch David set me up. The bar exam is a curve. He knows I am a better student and a faster one. He knows I will get all of the California law stuff a lot faster than he will. He deliberately and with premeditation sent me to a place where I would be torn from my studies by the succulent asses of nubile blond nymphets in skimpy track shorts.

Fuck David. I call and find out the Huntington Library in Pasadena has the same weekend hours. I spend the next four weeks studying the law of inheritance and the dissolution of the marital community among Pasadena matrons establishing the genealogy of their English watercolors. I feel good about the test. You only have to answer 13 of 15 essay questions and I just skip the one on community property. I run into David in the bathroom at the Long Beach auditorium on the second day of the exam when I have to take a piss during the multiple-choice part. He looks bad – like he has been puking.

THE ENFORCER

First day of work.

I am still a little nervous about the bar exam results. "Forget, it," I say to myself. I don't have a bad track record with tests – particularly tests taken by thousands of other vicious competitive types at the same time.

Like elephant hunting during the late Cro-Magnon period, competition only seems to improve my aim.

I meet my five "classmates." They all have on blue suits of varying shades. This includes the women. I thought I was all done with high school, but I am starting to think high school is a metaphor for the rest of your life.

I meet the office manager. She is very effusive and wearing a short polyester suit so I get occasional glimpses of her underwear, which is beige and lacy and not unappealing.

I meet my secretary. Lisa is a stringy bottle blond - very earnest.

She lives in Glendale, where the inhabitants not only subscribe to the *Ladies Home Journal*, but actually follow the recipes.

Lisa seems very concerned that my files look nice. She is happy that I don't have a strict file system so that she can be the one to organize them – making them "all beautiful." We are close to the turn of the decade and our firm management has decided that the more we spend on machines, the less we need to spend on people. I share Lisa with a partner.

I knock on the partner's door to introduce myself, making sure my jacket is on. My father told me that when you leave your office, you put on your jacket. Victor Aff ray turns out to be an affable guy. He is in his late forties with sandy hair. Very little grey. He has lots of pictures of blond adolescents in track shorts hitting things with rackets and bats.

"Your children?" I ask diplomatically.

"Three girls," he sighs. "Listen. I'm a trial lawyer, Richard. I'm not a litigator. I go to court. This is the real law. We don't draft contracts. We establish their meaning. You and I should do a few cases together. You would learn something."

"Yes, Sir. Mr. Affray." There is no point in mentioning I am a tax lawyer. Small talk is over. Back to work.

I soon discover that Mr. Affray is a very highly structured individual. Over a sandwich with a few second years at lunch, I discover he is known within the firm as "Affray the Enforcer." His principal client is a housing complex in North Hollywood, which was built as a tax shelter for some studio executives. In other words, the affable Mr. Affray practices eviction law on those without property at the behest of the propertied class. It seems that in order to fill up the housing complex some time back, the studio slumlords signed some pretty good long-term deals. The market changed and like any rich person they are trying to get out of the leases so they can rent for more money. Hence, the need for "Affray the Enforcer." Within the firm, Affray's legal judgment is sought regularly on the issue of how much you can get away with before being held in contempt of court by a particular superior court judge.

On day two, I notice Lisa is busily typing a motion to disqualify counsel to one of the soon to be evicted tenants of North Hollywood Towers.

"That's a little unusual," I say to Lisa.

"No. We do this on every case," Lisa says. "Mr. Affray says it is very important to set the tone right at the beginning."

I notice that the grounds for disqualification of counsel are that he has a master charge card issued by the same bank that holds the mortgage on the housing complex. This is not aggressive lawyering. It is certifiable, foam-on-the-mouth craziness.

I also soon learn that Mr. Affray has a very structured approach to explaining female behavior.

On day four, Mr. Affray summons me into his office. A quick look at his bookshelf indicates that his reading is limited to the California Code of Civil Procedures and books that one can buy in an airport bookstore with a swastika on the cover.

"Watch out for Lisa. She is very crabby. She is having her period."

"Yes, Mr. Affray."

"I'm working on a new case. Very exciting. It involves forgery on a twenty-year lease. How would you like to help out? We can even get you into court on a motion."

I am starting to figure out Mr. Affray's program. He is planning on sending me on a suicide mission in front of a superior court judge who's trying to disqualify some solo practioner on the grounds that he once used the restroom in our office building. When the judge sanctions me, Mr. Affray will claim that his junior associate is just being a little too aggressive and failed to seek his own mature judgment before making such arguments.

"Corporate guys have me pretty busy – lot of changes in the tax code," Mr. Affray.

"It's your loss."

Day ten I get another wave into Mr. Affray's office.

"Watch out for Lisa. She just broke up with her boyfriend."

"Thanks for the tip, Mr. Affray."

In the next few months, I find out that the menstrual cycle and ruptures in relations with boyfriends explains the entire range of female behavior. The operative rules governing female behavior do not seem to apply to his three daughters.

I also find out Mr. Affray drives a brand new red Porsche 911.

Structure has its rewards.

BUNKER HILL BABE

I am now at it for about a month. I have determined definitely that Cheryl is the second best typist in the firm.

The absolute best is Eva von Helfstein.

It is rumored that Eva's IBM electric required special modification at the IBM factory or the ball couldn't keep up with the input from her fingers. Another rumor says the ball had even melted down half way through an indenture, but I dismiss that rumor as just fanciful.

Eva, however, works for the managing partner and requires one week advance booking. And I am in a crisis and Cheryl is all that is available on one day's advanced notice.

Cheryl performs her assigned duties admirably. Somebody in New York had come up with the idea of structuring acquisitions by using multiple subsidiaries. That meant that all of the corporate formalities had to be scrupulously respected. That meant that some lowly tax associate, namely me, had to produce sets of minutes approving what is in essence the same transaction over and over again for each juridical person. Moreover, they had to be typo free or some idiot junior partner would find each and every one and probably ding me for lack of attention to detail. I would get a much smaller bonus at year end and, more importantly, I would fall behind in the competition with the five other associates that had graduated from Law School the same year I had.

I am feeling an above normal level of hatred towards my masters as my very tasteful thin gold wristwatch says 11:30 pm and the coffee is getting to be undrinkable sludge. Cheryl is still cheerfully retyping and I am making small talk.

Cheryl advertises that she lives in the only condo project in downtown Los Angeles. It is due west of the Arco towers. You can walk there.

Cheryl has now cheerfully retyped some of these idiot minutes three times. My prior impression of Cheryl is that her eyes were too close together. Watching the next set of corrections over her shoulder, I notice that she has rather perky breasts under her silk-looking, but actually polyester blouse.

The observation is confirmed when Cheryl sits on one of my two regulation courtesy chairs waiting for now the fifth set of revisions. "Courtesy" chair is what the office manager calls them. I still can't figure out what is courteous about the circa-1960s new age upholstery. Cheryl's red skirt hikes up revealing a rather inviting set of thighs and a glimpse at a pair of white lace panties. From the waist down, Cheryl is also a babe.

At this point I just give up on typos. I figure I would have a couple of hours in the morning to check typos when the deal closed anyway.

"You've been a huge help," I say.

Cheryl smiles – definitely a babe.

"You want dinner?"

Cheryl smiles again.

Dinner turns out to be Italian somewhere mid-Wilshire. It's open surprisingly late. We both start drinking Chianti. Cheryl is getting very talkative.

Marital status: divorced. Reason for divorce: married an older guy who was big into wife swapping. Verdict on wife swapping: much more exciting for the guy – most of these guys are pretty out of shape. Aspirations: unclear – lots of cosmetic surgery, which, according to Cheryl, is a good tax deduction. Financial plan: owns her own condo, works lots of overtime, and saving for an uncertain future. Drive on the way back to Bunker Hill Condo: my hand on her thigh. Conversation: limited to "you are cute."

Second act after dinner. Elevator to her apartment: very inspired groping starting in the lobby when the doorman is looking the other way. I run my hand under her skirt and then under the white panties –

no resistance, only moaning. Entry into the apartment: vaguely tasteful, no porcelain figures or cats.

Announcement by Cheryl: I need to slip into something more comfortable. The last time a woman said that to me after a hot date in Cherry Hill she reappeared in a pair of cut off jeans and a tank top. Result: great joy on my part.

Cheryl appears with pink negligee complete with see–through matching panties, straddles me and thrusts pert, and now I know high priced, breasts in my face. The matching panties end up on the white shag carpet and we end up locked in passionate fornication on the wall to wall. I am playing alpha doggie.

Next act: retire to bedroom. Cheryl produces a very large vibrator. It's bigger than a turkey drumstick. Cheryl pleasures herself in a rather inspirational manner while I languish in my refractory period. Third Act: Recovery. More passionate fornication. Drift off into sleep.

The next thing I know my very tasteful thin gold wrist watch says 6:30 am. I remember there is nothing worse than a cheap Chianti hangover. Somehow I make it back to my apartment while traffic starts getting vicious, get dressed in my best blue "close a deal" suit and get back to work and station myself in the board room shortly before 8:00 am.

I find more typos before the junior partner begins his review of the documents.

Cheryl gives me a knowing smile when she types the sixth set of revisions.

I think she looks pretty good for having bounced around on my member for most of the night. The wife swapping thing must have been good practice.

YOU CAN'T GO HOME AGAIN

It was a huge mistake to fuck Kristen.

Kristen is my old life. It is a relationship that should have ended in New York City, necking in a doorway to in an abandoned building in Soho in the shadow of a skyscraper. She was Long Island, NYU law school. I am not sure what she is doing in LA. She is probably running away from something, just like I am. However, LA is not a good place for young women given to linear thinking.

Kristen talks real fast. She smokes even more than I did.

Kristen is what I would call quasi assimilated. She has been in LA for eighteen months straight. She does not seem to suffer remorse. She has a little red MG. She has a rent controlled apartment with an ocean view in Santa Monica. And she has attitude. She is also easy.

Kristen is a litigator. This is the same genus of attorney to which my father belonged. They are fundamentally unhappy by nature, have no views other than in opposition to those of opposing counsel and generally treat life like some kind of game with a complicated scoring system employed only by them, which nobody else understands.

I get press ganged by the ASSIGNING PARTNER into helping out on some massive antitrust case that Kristen is working on full time. This puts me in the subordinate role. I ask questions politely about who exactly our client is so that I don't inadvertently produce any memorandum written by the idiots who populate the law department of our client. This puts Kristen in a superior position, which seems to make her very hot and bothered.

At 9:00 pm with many more boxes of documents to go before we sleep, Kristen suggests that we go to dinner. Dinner is Hamburger Hamlet around the corner. There are many drinks.

Somehow, Kristen manages to drive South on the Santa Monica freeway at 11:30 pm. She keeps the top up, but the heater on. I remember reading an article that Richard Nixon regularly built a fire in his house in San Clemente while running the air conditioner.

I am dizzy, but I can manage to negotiate my way through a labyrinth underground parking structure, carefully following the ass on Kristen's blue tailored suit. We reach her apartment on the third floor. Kristen produces a 750 milliliter bottle of Stolichnaya vodka from the freezer. A quick glance shows that the only other container stored therein is a dented, and apparently mostly empty, quart of Ben & Jerry's Tropical Rain Forest ice cream. The porch is small, but it has an unobstructed ocean view. Kristen produces a blanket, but no glasses. It is cold. We snuggle under the blanket and take turns swigging vodka out of the bottle. I can hear waves and it is remarkably peaceful.

I feel a little melancholy. Maybe this is a kindred spirit.

"We are both refugees here," I say.

I am thinking this sounds a little too "Hotel California" to be a really successful seduction line, but what the hell. All the really big issues in life are celebrated in popular song. The naked truth is that we are now both living in a culture where Marshall McCluen is a heavy dude. Her urban sensibilities seem to be even duller than mine. Of course, she has lived in this wasteland way longer than I have. I make eye contact.

"The question is whether the exile is self-imposed?"

"Yes, Yes," Kristen says.

I can't believe she has muttered assent to a line worthy of Marshall Mcluen.

I notice now that she is totally blotto.

Kristen is not interested in social commentary whether of the rock or poetical variety. She takes my hand and starts rubbing it on her crotch. Her man tailored skirt hikes up obligingly to her panty hose and she is breathing heavily with her mouth open.

I am not sure what overcomes me, but I unzip my pants under the blanket, pull out my cock, and grab Kristen's head firmly by the hair on the nape of her neck. Her mouth remains open in anticipation. I shove my now erect member in her mouth and she starts noisily sucking it. Kristen sticks her ass up in the air and I slap it a few times. I hear more frequent moans.

I now realize why Kristen has chosen employment in downtown Los Angeles in a profession that views its female members as a cross between fourteen-year-old factory workers and accomplished hookers. Kristen has very deep-seated masochistic tendencies.

I drag her to the bedroom, rip off her panty hose and pull her into bed. She pulls me on top of her and I enter her.

The effect is electrifying.

"Fuck me. Oh my God. Fuck me."

She is literally screaming.

I put my hand over her mouth to muffle the sound. Apparently she likes that too.

She continues to scream.

"Fuck the shit out of me." This is now repeated like a mantra. Thank God she has now dropped the "Oh my God."

Now somebody is banging on the wall. It sounds like a broom handle.

"I'm going to call the fucking police," a highly annoyed, but muffled voice says.

All of this background static is really interfering with my concentration. I concentrate on lunging and Kristen does not cooperate. Instead, she goes into full body contractions. Blessedly, she is clenching her teeth and is quiet except for low squealing.

I decide to omit the orgasm on my end. I am making mental notes of what I say to the investigating police officers. I wonder whether there will be two of them.

Kristen seems very relaxed. We share a cigarette.

"My neighbors hate me," she smiles.

I am wondering how sexually active Kristen is.

Saturday morning. I have a headache. Russian vodka is never a good idea. I remember reading that Soviet officials in the 1950s would float peppercorns on the top of a glass to drag the impurities down to the bottom. I notice that Kristen's bedroom is strewn with clothing from the week before. Her idea of housekeeping is to keep the freezer stocked with only essential items.

Kristen shows up with a not too clean glass with ice and more vodka.

"You can't be serious," I say.

"I've got a beer if you want that."

"This is alcoholism," I say.

"Takes the edge off," she says.

Breakfast in Venice and back to work.

Kristen is looking OK in jeans. I notice she is not wearing a bra. Sheer provocation. I make a mental note to be particularly abusive to her breasts that evening.

We make it through another ten boxes of documents.

Very soon a routine develops. Strangers searching for comfort in ritual. We start on the balcony looking at the ocean. I slip my hand down the back of her pants. Kristen's breathing gets a little more intense. I grab her hair and force her to her knees. She opens her mouth in anticipation. I stick my penis in her mouth and force her head down on it. She becomes more excited and we end up in bed – strictly missionary position with a lot of screaming. I can usually manage an orgasm when she calms down, which takes a while.

It's Saturday and we are sharing a cigarette in her clothes-strewn bedroom.

"Sex, ok?" she asks.

"Yeah, great."

"You want to experiment?" I realize that this is conversation I am having solely because Kristen is from New York. If she was like any girl I had dated thus far in LA, I would be describing my requirements, not having a discussion.

"You want to tie me up?"

"Would you like that?"

"I don't know."

I had forgotten that in New York there is a lot of pillow talk without much action. In California weird sex acts are the stuff of the next screenplay, and are accordingly taken very seriously. I wasn't going to be able to use a stick of butter to lubricate Kristen's ass before I butt fucked her. There was nothing in her refrigerator but Vodka and Ben & Jerry's.

I did buy 100 feet of clothes line in a hardware store on Third Street in Santa Monica, but it sits in the back of the Rabbit for two weeks.

I get up the next Sunday Morning, leave Kristen in bed breathing very heavily and take a walk down to the beach. There with the rising sun. It dawns on me that Kristen is perfectly happy with a diet that consists solely of sex in the missionary position with the promise of something nastier at some indefinite date in the future and subpoena responses punctuated with burgers washed down by Russian barter goods. In other words, I was dating somebody who, with a little less angst, could have been me. However, I am thinking that Narcissism is not my thing.

I decide to appeal to Kristen's rationality.

"Kristen, this isn't going anywhere, at least not anywhere good. We are using each other to try to avoid dealing with LA," I say.

"Two tie ups," Kristen responds.

"No, I am serious. I say."

Kristen pouts. The pout turns into a whine and the whine becomes an argument. The law may be a harsh mistress, but Hell still hath no fury like a women scorned.

Kristen does end up as a sort of friend, at least someone I talk to in a friendly way. But, before the talk, we still fuck now and then.

FRONTIER JUSTICE

It does not take long for me to discern that the first principle of social organization at the law firm of Snodgrass & Pecham is that any social difficulty can be dissolved in alcohol – the more difficult the social problem, the higher the quantity and proof.

The firm has a long-standing social outing in Santa Barbra where common themes such as greed and overwork are celebrated and strengthened. The high point is a state of the firm address where our MANAGING PARTNER — a sort of portly gentlemen with white hair plastered down to cover an increasing expanse of forehead — reads from a list of financial results. This produces applause among the crowd. This is the good news. Of course, it is followed by a series of graphs placed on the overhead projectors, detailing how such results would never be obtained again – except through the miracle of rabid overwork and aggressive poach of other lawyers' clients.

I have work to do and I end up driving up by myself to Santa Barbra in the cobalt blue Rabbit. I do charge the client for parking – what we associates call punitive billing. Kristen is guide for the first part of this extravaganza and I end up in some side bar with a bunch of litigators doing tequila shooters and pledging fealty to the MANAGING PARTNER.

Unfortunately, I find that the combination of lack of sleep and tequila have substantially impaired my powers of speech. When I can count ten used lime wedges at my place at the bar, I decide that it is a good idea to find my room.

This is a task that takes considerable concentration given my current condition and takes some time to accomplish – including spending some twenty minutes locked up in a service stairwell. I collapse into bed and when the room stops whirling around I sleep. I am having a very pleasant dream about a blond who was quite insistent that she needed a severe spanking when the telephone makes annoying noises.

"Where are you?" Kristen asks.

"I'm in bed."

"You are supposed to be here at dinner."

"Shit."

"Well, your absence has been noticed."

"You're just saying that because you miss me."

"I guarantee your absence will be noticed shortly. They can give you directions to the dinner at the font desk."

"OK. Don't be so harsh."

I hang up. I throw some cold water on my face, put on a blue blazer, and reflect that my liver still works well enough to purge enough Mexican pollutants out of my blood stream to allow rational thought after six hours. I am actually sober.

The directions are vague. I am on a stretch of the 101 and not clear whether my trajectory is North or South. I am driving cautiously.

I see a flashing light behind me. I pull over.

The officer is dressed like a Nazi storm trooper. He is wearing khaki instead of brown and he has a little bear on his sleeve instead of a swastika. The motto reads Eureka and not Gott mit uns. However, these niceties are lost on me.

"Is there a problem, officer?" Already, I can't believe that I am dumb enough to say that. The guy probably hears this same line thirty times a day.

"License and registration."

"Sure. But, what's the deal?" Nice recovery, I am thinking. It least I sound a little more native.

"You made an illegal lane change."

"An illegal what?"

"An illegal lane change. You changed lanes too quickly. I am going to write you up."

At this point Officer Schickelgrueber disappears into the safety of his squad car and leaves me to contemplate my hungover visage in the rear view mirror. When my tasteful gold wristwatch shows that twenty minutes have elapsed, I have the thought that I can at least help Officer Shickelgrueber find the relevant code section for an illegal lane change so that he can write me up and I can get to my dinner and avoid ending my career. I am pretty sure that an illegal lane change is not as serious as most traffic offences and that I am not going to have to do community service.

Resolute in my new attitude towards positive community-police relations, I get out of the car and walk towards Officer Shickelgrueber's police cruiser, which seems to have flashing lights everywhere.

Bad idea.

Officer Shickelgrueber is crouched behind the open door to his police cruiser. Through the open window, he has very large caliber automatic weapon pointed at my rapidly beating heart.

"Drop to your knees and raise you hands."

I comply immediately. Strong survival instincts make me ignore the fact that I will damage the knees of my only pair of grey dress trousers on the asphalt.

Exactly at this moment in time and space, no fewer than six cars full of associates from Snodgrass & Pecham drive by my exact location on Route 101. The driver of the first car slows down. In his eyes, I see the drunk look of surprise - his recognition that the individual with his hands in the air, submitting before the barrel of a storm trooper's weapon is not only known to him, but a fellow associate. As if in slow motion, I see the other passengers in the next five cars go through the exact same process of recognition and shock.

However, this episode of *CHiPs* has yet to reach its final act.

"I need to frisk you," says Officer Shickelgrueber.

"Sure thing." Something tells me that being absolutely compliant is good.

"Standard police procedure."

"Understand completely."

Officer Shickelgrueber seems to relax after he has verified that I have nothing on my person but a wallet with a ten-dollar bill in it.

"I am a lawyer," I say. "I was just going to offer to help find that code section on the illegal lane change."

"I can't seem to find the darn thing."

"Give me the code."

A code is a code. It has a certain logic. Tax is not highway conduct, but there is a logic. It takes me three minutes.

"Thanks," says Officer Shickelgrueber.

I have a yellow summons in my glove compartment and I am a half hour late. I try to slip into the restaurant while everybody is chomping down on their Cobb salad.

I almost reach my assigned place, when the big-mouthed MID-LEVEL LITIGATION PARTNER stands at his place, raises his glass and says:

"A toast to Mr. Parker, who has braved real adversity to be with us this evening." The entire firm breaks into applause.

Actually, the whole incident seemed to enhance my reputation. After all, how many downtown layers have had a bead drawn on them by the guy from *CHiPs*. Everybody simply assumed I was drunk and disorderly, which was the whole purpose of the weekend anyhow. I am now the poster boy for firm bonding.

The following Monday, I ask the MID-LEVEL LITIGATION PARTNER for a referral for a criminal lawyer in Santa Barbara.

"It will cost you," he says.

"I'm pissed," I say.

"No guarantees in trial work," he says. I am thinking that this guy's reputation as Mr. Sue and Settle is well deserved.

Another *bad idea*.

The Perry Mason of Santa Barbara demands a $250 retainer. He tells me the chances were 90-10 that Officer Shickelgrueber would not show up and the charges would be dismissed.

He is wrong.

Not only does Officer Shickelgrueber show up, he remembers all of the details, including the need to draw "his weapon" at the suspected perpetrator and "pat him down." He is not as expansive on my help in finding the relevant statutory citations to assist him in writing out the charges filed against me. I see the Judge glaring at me like some out of town mafia hit man. Things are clearly not going well.

Perry Mason makes it worse. He cross-examines Officer Shickelgrueber on the blind spot theory. I think I see him pick up a file that had somebody else's name on it. The Judge asks me if I have anything to say before I am sentenced.

I tell him I thought the arresting officer was very polite.

The fine was $35.00.

I am pretty sure the fine would be the same if I had said, "Fuck the pigs."

I drive back to LA. It is a two-hour drive. I think lawyers are scum.

The next day the MID-LEVEL LITIGATION PARTNER asks me how everything went in Santa Barbra.

"I fought the law and the law won," I say.

THE HEBREW PERSUASION

The ASSIGNING PARTNER shows up in my office. He is very chipper.

"Got a great real estate project for you."

"I'm a tax lawyer." I am trying very hard not to sound annoyed.

"Breadth of experience is something the firm greatly values."

"OK. OK. Who do I see?"

"Ernie Conner is waiting for you."

I've already been through this dance. I know exactly what THE ASSIGNING PARTNER is going to say and he knows the response. The only certain conclusion is that the work is going to get done. We are both sitting on the thirtieth floor of a very large building. The landlord is going to be paid. The most junior guy is going to do the work. These are the rules. LA rules.

Mr. Conner is an old timer. He is the head of the real estate department. I talked to him at the first firm cocktail party. Not just a dinosaur, but a real fossil out of a distant archeological period when the world was not yet covered in ice. His office is huge and he has various branding irons and other nasty looking ranch implements attached to the wall. I assume he is fond of the Los Angeles that existed before a bunch of guys, like me, with Ivy League degrees moved in. I guess he is going for the authentic western look.

I am doing my best to look earnest and not like a carpetbagger.

"Mrs. Robinson needs your help," he says.

"Plastics."

"I'm sorry?" He looks genuinely confused.

"Bad joke."

"Mrs. Robinson is one of the firm's oldest clients. For many years, she operated a very exclusive summer camp for young girls on a ranch in Arizona. She is up in years and is retiring and selling the ranch."

I'm thinking it's better to sell the ranch than buy the farm, but I am not going to make any more jokes. Mr. Conner is interested in branding irons, not standup. This is Flower street, not Sunset.

"Yes, Sir," I say respectfully.

"She needs help with the contract of sale."

"Where is the ranch?"

"In Arizona, somewhere near Flagstaff."

"But, Mr. Conner, I'm a California lawyer. I am not admitted to practice in Arizona."

"Richard, don't badger me with details. Janet needs our help."

Mrs. Robinson does need help. The contract of sale had been drafted by some East Coast land speculator types. It contains a seemingly endless set of provisions that allowed very substantial deductions from the purchase price. I spend hours on the telephone with the very nice lady at California Land Title and found that I could insure around most of these nasty contingencies. I spend a lot of time worrying about the ones I can not.

Oral easements keep bothering me. I can't insure against those. The land title lady is very clear about that. Even a box of grape jelly donuts do not produce a referral to another insurance company that would underwrite that risk.

I go to see Mr. Connor of the late Paleolithic period and sought his advice.

"Why don't you make a house call?" he says.

I do.

It is not a short drive to Palos Verdes, even though I leave downtown at 10:00 am. I pull up to a split level that looks like it was straight off the set of *Leave it to Beaver*. Trouble with LA is that these houses *are* often the set of something. You can never be sure that your subconscious mind is *not* playing tricks and might be right. There is a large portrait of Mr. Robinson. Judging from the width of his tie, he passed on some time ago.

"Have you given any easements to anybody to the camp?" I ask after two sips of tea and complimenting Mrs. Robinson on her remarkable collection of Hummel figurines.

"Easements?"

"Easements are just rights of access. Does anybody have the right to come across your property?"

Mrs. Robinson is still looking blankly at me. Must be more concrete, I think.

"Do any of the local ranchers up there drive their cattle across your property to water them?"

I am very proud of myself. I see the beginning lines of comprehension in Mrs. Robinson's face. I am getting into the whole ranch thing. I am humming the theme song to "Rawhide."

"No, it is very mountainous."

"Nobody rides across your property. Nobody at all?"

"Just the Sheriff."

"The Sheriff?" Now, I am humming "I shot the Sheriff." I can't get it out of my head.

"The Sheriff has a patrol that he sends over there to look for strays."

I call the Sheriff. I get the Deputy. Now I am humming, "I swear it was in self-defense."

He sounds like one of those guys on "Sky King."

"Well, we got trail rights over there," the Deputy says.

"Can you get up there any other way?"

"Why?"

"Well, Janet Robinson wants to sell her ranch and retire. She's a nice lady."

The Deputy grunts assent.

"Well, the Grump ranch takes you up the same mountain."

"That would be good. You call me when you talk to those folks."

I am glad it was a short conversation. This was the longest period of sustained countrified communication that I had ever experienced.

The Sheriff called a few days later.

"I signed that paper you sent me. The Grump folks are ok with us using their ranch."

The same day the fossilized partner stopped by.

"Janet is very happy."

"I'm very happy."

"I was a little worried when they told me that they had a tax guy on this project - but you're OK."

"You're OK, too." I already realize this sounds lame.

"A head's up, Janet is going to invite you to lunch."

Sure enough, two days after the closing with the East Coast land speculators and their overly shined wing tips, I am having lunch with Janet at the Brown Derby on Wilshire Boulevard.

Small talk with Janet is easy, and made increasingly easier by the fact that she expected me to drink alcohol. She eats some kind of chopped salad. I have raw meat. We are both chomping down on our berries, when Janet summons over the waiter.

"Young man," she says.

I notice the waiter has got to be pushing 60.

Janet hands the poor guy her MasterCard. I note it has a picture of a stagecoach on it.

"The service was very good. I want you to give yourself a good tip – five per cent."

"Yes, ma'am."

Apparently this is not unusual at the Brown Derby.

The nitty gritty financial details being disposed of, Janet turns her attention to me.

"May I ask you a personal question, Richard?"

"Of course, Janet. I am your lawyer."

"Are you of the Hebrew persuasion?"

For a moment, I freeze. I could be in Los Angeles in 1934. I inspect Janet's blue rinse hairdo and her carefully applied lipstick. There is nothing sinister. She doesn't even know what a Semite is - let alone an anti-Semite. She is simply an artifact from a different time and place.

"I suppose you could say that, Janet."

"Good."

"Good?"

"I wanted to introduce you to my head counselor. She is of the Hebrew persuasion too."

The light goes off. Jane told me her family raises poodles. She is not going to have any random acts of intercourse pollute the bloodline.

"I thought I could have you both over for Easter dinner."

The thought of resurrection is less disturbing than a giant ham studded with cloves in geometric patterns on a plate imprinted with vestigial Hummel figures.

"Janet, may I be frank?"

"Of course, Richard. You are my lawyer."

"These are different times. I think it might be better if you just gave me her telephone number and I will give her a ring and have coffee."

"Whatever you think is best."

Mandi lives in a weird apartment building in Santa Monica with portholes instead of windows. It could be the nautical motif or it could have beeen some ship building firm in Long Beach was having a liquidation sale. It is Los Angeles, after all, and you can really never be absolutely sure.

Mandi opens the door. She is a blond with long hair. She is wearing very small pink track shorts. No shoes. She has pink polish on her toenails.

"White wine?"

"Great."

Mandi hates her father. That is the same guy who wrote a check for $500,000 in cash for a two bedroom condo with an unobstructed view of the Pacific Ocean and white shag carpets. I am thinking about having a vasectomy. This is not a good place to breed if you want affection from your children.

"You smoke?"

"Great." I am pretty sure Mandi is not talking about the Marlboro man. I am being unusually reserved, but I figure you can't go that wrong by uttering positive expletives every couple of minutes and pretending to listen carefully.

Mandi produces a hash pipe made out of a steer horn. Must be the Arizona influence.

"Great stuff," I say. I am still focusing on the positive.

Mandi takes a huge hit and giggles.

"I like you. I was expecting some uptight jerk when Janet called me. I mean Janet is such an old lady."

"Well, thanks," I say.

"Excuse me," she says.

Mandi returns. She is wearing a dog collar and a pair of high heel shoes with ankle straps with little heart shaped locks. They are both black. Otherwise she is stark naked. I notice that she has shaved off most of her pubic hair, except for a tiny little heart shaped patch on top. Clearly we have a theme. Next to the *mons veneris* is a butterfly tattoo. In one hand Mandi is holding a neatly coiled 100 foot length of clothes line and in the other a bowie knife. We are definitely not in Palos Verdes any more and what is going to happen next has nothing to do with Hummel figurines.

"I want you to tie me up and fuck me," Mandi says. She sounds very serious and puts an album of Vangelis' greatest hits.

My first thought is that they are not big on foreplay in Santa Monica, but I did win the knot tying contest at the 1964 Boy Scout Jamboree in Valley Forge, Pennsylvania. To the theme song of Blade Runner, I force Mandi to lean over the rather tasteful retro couch, run the clothes line through the convenient ring in her dog collar and anchor her legs a nice distance apart on the back two legs of the couch with the remaining line. In keeping with the "foreplay is for sissies theme," I slap her ass a few times and mount her from the rear. Mandi lets out a series of short moans. When I count five organisms, I climax.

I cut Mandi loose. She produces a cigarette, lights it and gives me a drag.

"I like being helpless," she says.

I decide at this point that my focus should be on non-verbal communication. I grab her hair, force her to her knees and shove my cock in her mouth. It is really just for show; no way am I going to come again. When I pull her head away, she looks very meaningfully in my eyes.

"You're cute," Mandi says.

The light outside on Third Avenue is blinding. It is 3:00 pm and I am barely functioning. Too many drugs and women who hate their fathers. There is no way I am going to get on the Freeway. Kristen's apartment is around the block and I know to a certainty that there will be vodka in the freezer.

I find the key under the doormat, drink a third of the bottle, and climb into Kristen's bed. I drift off to sleep, thinking that Mandi was too weird for a long-term relationship, although it seems like a shame to let it go after a single one-afternoon-stand. Still, if she has to be trussed up on date one, something tells me that date two could reach hospital emergency room status. Not a career-enhancing move, I decide. Date two is postponed without a date, as we say in the law biz.

MY MENTOR

Somewhere on the 34th floor of the same building where my one window office is located, a bunch of middle class, no class guys are plotting my future. The personnel committee determins to assign me a mentor. I just don't know about it — yet.

On the first Monday in January, I get a glimpse of the plan that has been carefully mapped out for me.

The ASSIGNING PARTNER drops by my office promptly at 10:00 am. It is one of those premeditated "I am in the neighborhood" drop-ins.

"Are you free for lunch?"

"Yes, sir."

"I have asked Bernie Lietman from the general practice group to join us."

"Great."

I immediately go next door and ask Kristen.

"Who is Bernie Lietman?"

"Scum," she says with considerable relish.

"What do you mean by scum?"

"Scum. Real pool slime. He represents women in divorce cases. From what I hear, they are mostly Scandinavian models. He tries to fuck them. He also tries to fuck every female associate in the firm who is smaller than he is. Thank God, there aren't that many of them."

I notice that Kristen is not quite 5'1".

Kristen gives me that catty laugh and the "just wait" look. The last time Kristen is this excited she told me a story about a MID LEVEL

PARTNER who was accosted in the stairwell by a naked paralegal who said that she loved him. Apparently, he still can't get an erection.

Lunch was at the Pacific Dining Car — noteworthy because it is both pricey and off-campus. Despite being surrounded by slabs of red meat, Mr. Lietman orders a turkey sandwich on rye bread

"I'll have that dry," he says.

Mr. Lietman orders a cup of hot water. Nothing is going to poison this guy's bodily essences.

Bernie needs only the briefest of introductions before he starts to hold forth on life, love and the law. It becomes clear to me that this guy thinks exactly like the Enforcer, except he evicts men from their conjugal bed rather than their low rent apartment with an ocean view.

"Richard, this is a great practice area. It is tax driven. It requires both deal skills and litigation skills. You also have to be psychologists — many of your clients are looking solely for revenge. You have to convince them that *the money* is the revenge." Bernie has this annoying habit of rubbing his hands together whenever he mentions the word money.

Bernie is so overcome with his own rhetoric, he has to pause and use his napkin to swipe a little fleck of drool off the side of his mouth. I'm starting to think that the dry turkey wasn't such a bad idea.

After lunch, I am assigned to work on Bernie's latest appeal. Seems Bernie had no luck busting the prenuptial agreement in the court below. Seems the judge just wasn't buying the testimony of Ellie, the 18-year-old Norwegian model with 38D knockers. Ellie is wife No. 3 of the guy who owned the biggest Mercedes dealership in Palos Verdes. I study the trial record. These people lived not in another county, but another planet.

Kristen stops by office late in the afternoon.

"Check out box 37."

"What do you mean?"

"Box 37 of the trial exhibits in the Lanstom case. Check it out. It's in storage."

It is too late in day.

I go to storage in the morning. I ask where the trial exhibits are for the Lanstom case. The clerk gives me a sort of knowing look and jerks his thumb to the corner. Box No. 37 is surprising easy to find. It is one of 120 boxes of documents produced by Mr. Lanstom, I know this much from reading the trial transcript.

Box 37 is far from full. It contains only 150 more or less Polaroid photographs of approximately 20 different young women posing with their legs spread wide open manipulating their genitalia with various vibrators of different colors and sizes. They are all seated on the same sheepskin rug.

Normally, pornography for me is not a bad turn on, particularly if followed very closely by nasty sex acts. Most of Mr. Lanstom's lady friends are either well endowed by the same plastic surgeon or appear very eager. I am wondering if Kristen wants to get me hot and bothered so I do her in the broom closet. However the repetition of the sheepskin rug under twenty different gaping vaginas leaves me worrying about the public health implication of this photographic record. My thoughts wander to Mr. Lanstom's dry cleaning bill and whether he should buy an autoclave to sterilize his dildo collection.

I end up working late. Kristen asks me about the pictures. I tell her. She is not bothered by my fears of infectious diseases and random speculations regarding whether they have sheep dips for rugs. She seems to get very hot and bothered. She keeps rubbing against my zipper on the way to the parking lot. I get a very inspired blow job in the back seat of the cobalt blue Rabbit, but at Kristen's insistence, I have to park it where one of the security lights had burned out in the second floor of the parking lot.

The next day, my mentor announces that we are going to someplace in Alabama that I never heard of in order to close a deal. Seems that divorce has forced the sale of the family chicken wire manufacturing plant. Bernie says that we have a lien on proceeds to pay the firm's fees. As such, this is a very important transaction.

We get on a Delta flight – two seats together in coach. I can tell this is going to be a painful trip. Bernie has brought two litigation bags. If you stack them up end on end, they are almost the same size as he is. Bernie hands me a set of title reports.

"Check the legal descriptions in the deeds against the title report."

"Yes, Sir."

I get to work. Bernie pulls out another set of files. The first is labeled "Lietco – Sunset". A quick glance to my side shows it is the limited partnership agreement for a thirty-unit condominium project. The general partner is no other than Bernie Lietman. Bernie asks the stewardess for a cup of hot water. Bernie is just getting warmed up. The second file is labeled "Lietco – Santa Monica." This appears to be a retail project on Santa Monica pier. General partner is Bernie Lietman.

Now it dawns on me. Bernie is billing Mrs. Lanstom to extract as much money from the philandering, pussy-photographing Mr. Lanstom as the California courts will allow while simultaneously minding his Los Angeles real estate empire, which stretches from the mountains to the ocean. I find myself overcome with admiration. I am sitting next to the Napoleon of Southern California real estate.

Alabama is a disaster.

The drawl is so thick, I can barely understand what is being said. Mr. Alabama keeps on saying that he is just a country lawyer, but in the meanwhile Bernie keeps giving away not only the chicken wire, but the chickens too. He clearly wants to get paid and contract details are "not withstanding," as we lawyers like to say. Bernie has a very clear focus and is clearly not letting his client's interest get in the way of closing this deal.

In the middle of the closing, somebody drives a forklift into an eight-inch water main. I receive a telephone call from the plant manager and tell the assembled group that there is now four inches of water on the plant floor.

"Well, you better get somebody over there to pump out your plant," drawls Mr. Alabama.

"It's your fucking plant," says Bernie. "We are closed."

"Hell, boy, you ain't got the money and we ain't closed," says the country lawyer.

Bernie is turning a deep shade of red and looks ready to explode. I have to do something.

"Fifty-Fifty," I say. "What can the damage be," I say. I'm going to write up a side letter.

Both sides retreat to their respective sides of the conference room and glower at each other. The letter is acceptable, the firm is paid, and Bernie and I catch an earlier flight home.

At the taxi stand at LAX, Bernie turns to me shortly before my cab left.

"That was good judgment," he says.

"Thank you, Sir. Good night, Sir."

It takes me a day, but I pen the first line of an opening appeals brief that reads:

"Ellie and Chuck met at the Bar of the Balboa Bay Club. A few days later, Chuck proposed marriage and Chuck insisted that they leave immediately in his Porsche for Las Vegas in order to be married. Ellie, a Norwegian citizen who was visiting relatives in Newport Beach, agreed. Chuck used a portable telephone to call Sam Feuerman, his lawyer. Sam presented Ellie with a 50 page prenuptial agreement. Ellie, who had a limited command of English, having completed only the equivalent of the twelfth grade in Oslo, asked what it all meant. Sam told Ellie that if the marriage didn't work out Chuck would get to keep his boat. Chuck then told Ellie that the traffic would be bad if they didn't leave immediately for Vegas and Ellie signed the document without reading a word of it – not that she would have understood a word.

"The sole issue for this Court is whether the State of California will recognize that unread and unexplained agreement as a legal and binding contract and will use its sovereign power to enforce each and every condition drafted by Mr. Feuerman even if their plain meaning fails to meet standard of unconscionability."

Bernie is impressed. I see him pursing his lips and reaching for a tissue when he gets to the sovereign power part.

I cut loose from Bernie a week later. He is clearly going to be bad news in even the short run. I have a nightmare about my mother finding Polaroid pictures of me while getting to know my new client base. The Internal Revenue Code was looking a lot better.

NASAL CONGESTION

Sam, Sam invites me to visit.

He lives in Orange County, which he told me is "due South" of Marina Del Rey. I steer the metallic cobalt blue Rabbit onto the 5 Freeway. I always seem to be able to find the 5 Freeway. I can't find much else. The Thomas Brother map book is a permanent fixture on the front passenger seat of the cobalt blue Rabbit. Somewhere around Long Beach Boulevard, I get off of the 405. It seems like I have been driving for hours.

"For Christ's sake," I am thinking, "I am probably in Mexico".

The guy in the Texaco station is amused by my question. I am relieved that he speaks English.

"Keep going South," he says.

"I've been driving south for hours."

"You from New York?" says the man with the star.

"Yeah, something like that," I say.

After an eternity of driving past the same intersection with the same Taco Bell (now offering the breakfast burrito), I find Sam, Sam's house on the Balboa Peninsula. He is living in what I would have called a row house, but one that has an all glass front, facing the beach. It has a view of the Pacific Ocean obstructed only by the sun umbrellas shielding sixteen-year-old blond bodies in string bikinis from a potential overdose of gamma radiation.

I open the sliding glass doors. A very bored-looking, somewhat older blond lady is sitting on a couch, which I discern is covered with a velveteen material designed to pick up the same squiggly line in the sculptured carpet. Ms. Very Bored is wearing only a tight white

T-shirt, which leaves her midriff exposed, and a florescent orange pair of panties. After all, the sign on the freeway did say, "Welcome to Orange County."

Ms. Very Bored is looking intently at a detergent advertisement on the television.

"Where is Sam?" I ask.

"Upstairs," she says.

My presence only seems to have increased her level of boredom. I am thinking that my track record with women with florescent orange underwear is not good.

Sam, Sam is shaving.

I sit on the waterbed, avoiding some suspicious-looking spots on the black sheets and pick up a copy of "Road and Track." It appears muscle cars are having a resurgence, as if in Southern California they had ever fallen out of favor.

Sam, Sam is fatter than at law school and quite animated. He wants to eat.

We end up at the Pacific Coast Diner and eat bacon and scrambled eggs. Cheri, the name attached to the florescent orange panties, has donned a pair of white short shorts for the occasion. Cheri leaves. She is not interested in manly chitchat over animal protein and has left for an "appointment." Sam, Sam informs me that she is a massage therapist. He also informs me that she gives the best hand job in Orange County.

So much for male bonding over short order food. We go back to Sam, Sam's place and sit on plastic chairs. I stare at the Pacific Ocean.

Sam, Sam produces a bottle of off -label Tequila and we drink. Tequila is a mistake. I start feeling nasty. The nastiness is directed at Sam, Sam.

How can this criminal, who but for the grace of God and Governor Moonbeam, should be working behind the counter in Circle K, just waiting to be the victim of an armed robbery, end up with the Pacific Ocean as a front yard and the hand job queen of Orange County as an Attendant?

"I'm getting into personal financial management," Sam, Sam says.

I take another slug of Tequila.

"What in the fuck is that?" I ask.

I'm thinking overt hostility might precipitate a change in topic or, at a minimum, a moment of silence.

Bad question. Sam, Sam is now boring me with details of finding apartments in Houston for some guy in Newport Beach who needs to disappear from the Hollywood crowd that he hangs with on the weekends. Seems like he needs a new apartment every month.

"Does he like women with big hair?" I say, trying to affect a little interest.

The Tequila is stripping away the edge and I am getting one of my recurrent urges to drive to 96th Street in Santa Monica and watch the planes leaving for New York. It is getting towards dusk and the sixteen-year-old blonds with the string bikinis have left the beach.

But the ocean is very calming and the sound of the waves is soothing. I am finding it easier to ignore Sam, Sam's ramblings and look at the dark green seaweed washing up on the shore.

"I need a nap," I say.

Sam, Sam reflects. Not that balancing two conflicting ideas comes to him very naturally anyway. It is clearly a more difficult exercise for him after a half a bottle of Jose Cuervo. Sam, Sam apparently decides that it would project a more suitable attitude if I am well rested for his guest.

I snuggle up with the blanket on the velveteen couch, thinking vaguely what unnatural acts may have occurred on it. I am weary from a week of commuting, communing with the internal revenue code and acknowledging Jose's latest contribution to my mental health. I fall asleep.

I wake up several hours later and try to find Sam, Sam. He is in the bathroom. This time he is doing lines of nose candy and insists that I do the same.

I haven't done this sort of thing before, so I observe carefully.

"Good shit," says Sam, Sam.

I am doing my best to make the identical snorting noises as Sam, Sam through a rolled up hundred. He smiles. I must be succeeding.

"Good shit," repeats Sam, Sam.

"Good shit," I say. I'm not stupid. I can take a cue.

"Holy shit," I think. I suddenly realize that I am now completely wired.

I am not thinking. I am incapable of thinking. I am feeling. I am feeling speed, power, and exhilaration. Sam, Sam pours more tequila.

Thank God. My friend Jose is a calming influence.

Sam has disappeared. I am now calm enough to survey the world outside of the bathroom.

On the waterbed, I see this perfect baby blue spandex ass beckoning to me from across the room. Spandex is not just a fabric, I think. It is a lifestyle. The perfect ass is attached to a perfect set of pear shaped breasts. On top of the breasts is a full head of blond hair. In the middle of the blond cloud is a red Betty Boop pair of lips and two dark pools of mascara. Was there lust before Maybelline?

My Peruvian super charged circulatory system is pumping blood into my member at an alarming rate. It is becoming large and uncomfortable. It needs relief.

I make contact with the dark, limpid pools.

"Hi," I say.

"Hi," says the red lips. The lips are just moving. They don't seem to be attached to anything else.

"Where's Sam?" I ask.

"He's on the phone to Houston. It's important," says the red lips.

"Oh," I say.

This is lame, I think.

Ms. Maybelline is going to start to babble, I think. I am going to lose the hard on of the century. My mind is racing. Wait. There are still four lines on the mirror on the vanity cabinet.

"Wanna do some great shit?" I ask.

"Sure," says the red lips.

I hand her the rolled up hundred. Snorting sounds. Line one gone. More snorting. Line two. I start rubbing my member up and down on the spandex ass. Freud says this shit gives you intellectual clarity and here I am behaving like a dachshund in heat. Line three gone. Now the spandex is gone, leaving only a beautiful expanse of tanned butt. My member is crying for release from its denim prison. Dry humping the formerly spandexed ass is making it worse. Line four gone. Now the red lips are at zipper level and showing their appreciation for the Peruvian aperitif.

I am still not sure how I made it to the waterbed. I remember vaguely timing my thrusting with the sound of the waves of the Pacific Ocean until I reached to point of relief. Then there are no more waves. There is only blackness.

Then there is light! Light is everywhere. Light is extremely painful. Is this just Jose getting even? I am not sure. My head hurts. But all of this is just a nuisance.

I can no longer breathe through my nose. This thought slowly overtakes my brain. I now hold a monopoly on all mucus production in Orange County. The stuff is literally dribbling out of my nostrils. Kleenex, shirt sleeves, nothing would arrest the flow. The god of the Incas has targeted me for human sacrifice.

I find my clothes and my car keys and I found CVS. I buy four Afrin nasal inhalers. The box says "Extra Strength." I find the San Diego freeway and I systematically snort all four on the way back to LA. I get to my apartment, pull the phone cord out of the wall and sleep until Monday at 5:45 am.

I still need to make three cups of very strong coffee to get to work.

MILLION DOLLAR BABY

Sam, Sam calls at about 10:00 am on Monday. I am actually feeling pretty good after the coffee. I am definitely ready to join the coffee achievers.

"What happened, man?" says the voice on the phone. "You just took off."

"I don't know," I say. "It is like a 'I had to get back to LA' thing."

"Julie did 200 dollars of my coke," says Sam, Sam. He sounded irritated.

"Who's Julie," I ask.

"Julie is my girlfriend who you fucked on Saturday night," Sam, Sam says. Now he sounds really irritated.

"Oh, sorry man, I'll send you a check today," I say.

"No problem," Sam, Sam says.

The financial details behind, Sam, Sam is now positively engaging.

"Come down next weekend. I'll have Julie over. She says she dug you, man. Julie can suck the chrome off a trailer hitch."

"I'll give you a call," I say, still sounding lame. I'm thinking that I still need to try to figure out this California car/sex unity thing.

After I hang up with Sam, Sam, I get in the elevator and walk down Flower Street. The nice thing about walking in downtown LA is that there are very few people on the street. I smoke three cigarettes. It is time to consider my life. I had just fucked one of my law school classmate's girlfriends in his water bed without knowing her name after getting her high on his cocaine in his bathroom in a place where every intersection had a Taco Bell (which sold burritos for breakfast). It isn't exactly an excuse that I hate Taco Bell and that Julie is just one of Sam, Sam's girlfriends. It also isn't exactly an excuse that Sam, Sam had fucked my girlfriend, and her girlfriend, at law school, at the same time, because it was before she was my girlfriend. And anyway, I had fucked Sam's sister to get even. I sincerely doubt that Julie "dug me" or could pick me out of a line up, even a line up where none of the suspects wore pants. My behavior did not bode well for the future. I am going to die of the mucus equivalent of a heart attack or contract some loathsome disease from Sam, Sam's couch. Moreover, as a first year tax associate, I couldn't be financing the consumption of nose candy for a progression of dyed blonds in Orange County without getting evicted from my apartment. Moreover, Sam, Sam, although fully pardoned by Governor Moonbeam, has a dark and dangerous criminal past. He had criminal thoughts and criminal tendencies. I need to stay far way from Sam, Sam and Orange County, or I too would turn down the criminal path.

I took the elevator, went back to my desk, had yet another cup of coffee and tried to lose myself in the tax code. Just in the middle of parsing one of the more self-contradictory revenue rulings issued in the past several years, Steve plops himself down at one of my visitor's chairs. Steve is from Boston. He is a regular, wholesome East Coast guy. I'm not really sure why he moved to Los Angeles, but it only took him four months to get engaged once he got here. His fiancée is from San Diego. She is nice. I met her once. She has a nice laugh and doesn't say much. She is pretty and has dark hair. She says "yes" after most of what Steve says.

"Gloria and I are having brunch in Santa Monica on Sunday," Steve says.

"That's nice," I say.

"Gloria thinks you would like her roommate. She's at UCLA too," Steve says.

The whole UCLA thing hits a nerve. A wholesome college girl? Not the gun moll of a crazed dope dealing criminal masquerading as a financial consultant in Disneyland? This is the right path – the path of a tax associate at an established downtown LA law firm. I see another path leading to a glorious future in the sunshine.

"I would love to," I say. I surprise myself. I actually *sound* enthusiastic.

"Great," says Steve. "Gloria will be really happy."

Sunday morning I appear at the appointed Mexican restaurant on 3rd Street in Santa Monica wearing a pair of khakis and a pink alligator shirt. I do put on socks. I still hope I am not overdoing it, but Steve is so preppy, I figure I can't out-prep him even if I tried.

A waitress dressed like some Mexican serving wench in a John Wayne movie escorts me to a table. Gloria is sitting with hunched shoulders looking like she has recently been beaten because she did not say "yes" enough. Steve is studying the menu like it's a Delaware Supreme Court opinion. Lonnie is talking to Gloria in a very animated manner.

"This is Lonnie," Steve says.

Lonnie is wearing a pink skirt and a black top with lots of ruffles. She is dressed for the venue. She has long brown hair and seems pretty nicely proportioned. I haven't gotten a full frontal view.

"Hi, Lonnie," I say. "I love your outfit."

"Pink is my favorite color," Lonnie says.

Thanks to my choice in shirts, we are off to a good start. I give Gloria one of those little LA air kisses and sit down. I am right about Steve. Topsiders. No socks and an alligator on his left tit.

"What's everybody having?" I say as cheerfully as I can.

Turns out nobody is having anything that I even would remotely consider eating. I order some kind of egg dish that sounds like a Latin American *latifundia*, which doesn't promise excessive amounts of either beans or guacamole. I am disappointed as it has a lot of both. Everybody else is pretending that it's dinner, although the sun is reaching the middle of the sky.

"I'm having a frozen margarita," Lonnie says with a nice laugh. I notice she is wearing lots of lip gloss.

"I'll have one those too," I say to John Wayne's ex-serving wench. I'm not exactly sure how to begin with Lonnie, so a little social lubrication seems in order.

"So you do tax," Lonnie says. "Steve says you are brilliant and all the corporate guys want you on their deals."

"Steve exaggerates," I smile.

I love these set ups, I am thinking. Not that this poor girl would even have the remotest idea of what a tax lawyer does, but Steve has filled his fiancé with stories of my brilliance and desirability. These fundamental traits have become even more exaggerated in hushed conversations in some entirely student occupied apartment building in West Los Angeles where the laundry room undoubtedly smells like mildew.

"So, Lonnie, you do psychology," I say.

I think of Stanford's admonition that the ideal in seduction is to use the woman's name in every sentence.

"Do you study Freud, Lonnie?"

"Not too much," says Lonnie. I am not convinced that she even knows that I am talking about the father of psychoanalysis. However, on the bright side, I notice that Lonnie has been attacking her margarita like a real trooper. I figure I can get a little risqué. I don't want her to think I am just another pink-shirted preppy.

"Do you study any deviant behavior?" I ask.

"Oh, yeah," Lonnie says. I have her interest.

She laughs and makes eye contact. I notice she is wearing blue eye liner.

"That's my favorite part of psychology," she says.

"Do you do any clinical studies, Lonnie?" I am not sure she is registering the word "clinical."

"Wow," says Lonnie. "This is really strong." She is rapidly draining the alcohol infused Slurpee through a straw and the rapidly declining level of her glass indicates that she is perilously close to a brain freeze.

"Eat some chips, Lonnie," I say. "You shouldn't drink too much on an empty stomach."

Lonnie eats some chips. The food comes. I push mine around on the plate for a while. Lonnie does the same. Steve and Gloria actually seem to be eating the green and brown muck. The mariachi band plays. The girls know the songs and sing along. I have to give the bandleader five bucks to go away. Who cares how hot the sun is anyway? More margaritas. A trip to the bathroom for Lonnie. Lonnie returns with fresh lip gloss. Steve announces that he and Gloria have to go and pick out silverware patterns. Gloria smiles. Steve smiles and seems very eager to pick out things for Gloria.

"Let's walk on Ocean Parkway, Richard," Lonnie says.

"Ok," I say. I am thinking of the song "Nobody Walks in LA."

Lonnie is walking very quickly down Ocean Parkway in Santa Monica. I am doing my best to keep up. Suddenly she approaches a young mother pushing a perambulator and peers inside. It all happens so quickly that I can't react.

"That's a million dollar baby!" she screams. "That's a million dollar baby!"

"Thank you," the apparent mother mutters.

"That's a million dollar baby!" Lonnie screams again.

"Very beautiful child," I mumble. I am hoping that nobody I know is anywhere near Santa Monica.

It is becoming abundantly clear to me that Lonnie wants children and that you can't exactly call her an anti-materialist. She can't seem to stop moving. At my insistence, we sit on a bench on Ocean Parkway. There are very few people on foot and all of them are old and look like they had just emigrated from Brighton Beach in Queens. Without tables and mariachi bands in the way, I can inspect Lonnie. She has a very trim, athletic body. She also appears to have some kind of aversion to natural fabrics. The sunlight reveals her skirt and ruffled top had their origins in a chemical plant in a part of New Jersey that even I had not visited. Finally, a moment of quiet. I am looking at Pacific Ocean and the sound of the waves is making me feeling calm. Lonnie is telling me how her father is a podiatrist in San Diego. I am sort of listening.

"You really like that deviant stuff, huh?" Lonnie asks.

This question snaps me back to attention. Did Lonnie look the word up? Did she ask Gloria what it meant in the Ladies room? Does Lonnie have some kind of foot thing? Or is kinky just what college girls in Southern California do?

"It's nice to try new things," I say. I realize I am sounding lame again. Lonnie puts her hand on mine and squeezes it. She has quite a grip.

"There are a few deviant things I'd like to try with you," she says.

"How about next Saturday for dinner," I say.

PLEASE BUZZ ME RE VARIOUS FUCK UPS

Los Angeles presents a confusing dialectic. Whenever my social life seems to start heading in the right direction, my career seems to teeter on the brink of disaster. I am almost through the mental process of freeing myself from the drug crazed gun molls of Orange County and the ASSIGNING PARTNER shows up in my office and gives me a litigation assignment.

The MID-LEVEL LITIGATION PARTNER is now my new master.

That, in itself, is not problematic. I have spent enough time with my father to talk a pretty good game about litigation, even if I hate the endless procedural jousting, but this guy is doing a corporate deal. In other words, the MID-LEVEL LITIGATION PARTNER is proving that his macho-ness spilled over from the courthouse into the boardroom and I can see problems at every turn, like, as an initial matter, the guy didn't have a clue about basic accounting.

Moreover, the "deal" is for one of his country club buddies who is buying a sorry collection of stripper wells in Signal Hill with dubious long term production potential, but a high promise of lasting environmental problems.

So, I soon find myself in a conference room on the 30th floor with a California Oil and Gas man. He is wearing a plaid jacket on which the stripes are at least two inches apart and in colors which could not be found on the paint wheel at Dunn & Edwards.

We are in the middle of some big time posturing.

"We are all done negotiating," says the MID-LEVEL LITIGATION PARTNER.

"Excuse me. We have some additional points," says the plaid jacket.

"I said we are all done negotiating." His tone is very aggressive

"Well, we would like to raise one or two additional points."

"You have no additional points." His tone is now hostile.

"Well just one or two points."

"Sign the contract, don't sign the contract or roll the contract up and shove it up your ass." His tone is now confrontational.

The MID-LEVEL LITIGATION PARTNER turns to me.

"Richard, we are leaving."

He turns to the two paid clad oil men.

"You have exactly ten minutes. Sign it or get the fuck out of here."

We are now in the hell.

"What do you think, Richard?" asks the MID-LEVEL LITIGATION PARTNER.

This, I think, is a very dangerous question. My boss has just told some polyester oil guy to commit sodomy with a legal document. His testosterone levels are so high that they are probably not measurable.

"I think that it is sometimes important to set limits and define consequences," I finally say, trying to sound as thoughtful as possible. One of my mother's friends in Hackensack used to say that all of the time. She taught second grade.

The MID-LEVEL LITIGATION PARTNER seems happy with the response.

When we go back in the conference room, the contract is lying in the middle of the table. It is signed. One of the polyester guys asks to have his parking ticked validated. I take care of it.

I am soon invited to lunch at the California Club with MID-LEVEL LITIGATION PARTNER.

"I studied zoology in college," says the MID-LEVEL LITIGATION PARTNER while eating his hamburger.

"Yes," I say politely.

"A lot of client conduct I find no different from some of the higher orders of apes," he says.

The next day is not going to be fun. I have to put together all of the schedules for the purchase and sale agreement. The detail is excruciating. I have to check production logs for each of these wells. Some of them produce less than eight barrels a day. I am driving down Olympic Boulevard and the oil light comes on. I drive into a Mobil station right outside of Korea town.

"Check the oil," I say.

The guy at the station nods and opens up the hood.

I am distracted. I am trying to remember whether I rechecked all of the payroll records, which have to be attached to the purchase and sale agreement. The guy looks like he is putting in oil. I hand him ten bucks and tell him to keep the change.

I decide to do the rest of the trip on the freeway. As soon as I get off the on ramp, the cobalt blue Rabbit shudders and then dies. I am now blocking three lanes of traffic and three hundred people are honking at me. I get out of the car and push it to the shoulder. I open up the hood. The motor is covered with oil. The oil cap is gone.

The guy in the tow truck is nice. He drops my car at the nearest dealer and me at a bus stop. This is the first time I have been on a bus in Los Angeles. I am a little self-conscious. I am wearing a brown suit. Both sleeves are black to the elbow.

When I get to work, there is a note on my desk from the MID-LEVEL LITIGATION PARTNER: "Good afternoon. Please buzz me re various fuck ups."

I grab the note and march to the MID-LEVEL LITIGATION PARTNER's office.

He is on the telephone. I sit in his courtesy chair and watch with some satisfaction as the oil slick spread on the arms of the chair. He finally gets off the phone.

"I resign," I said.

Needless to say, my resignation was not accepted. Apologies were made all around.

I get my review a few weeks later.

"The MID-LEVEL LITIGATION PARTNER felt that some of your behavior was manic-depressive," said the associate's committee guy.

"Can I get a second opinion?" I ask.

IN LOS ANGELES, YOU ARE WHAT YOU DRIVE, BUT SOMETIMES THE DRIVER IS IRRLEVANT

I suspect that the MID-LEVEL LITIGATION PARTNER may have been criticized for his use of a medical diagnostic code in reviewing one of the hardest working associates in the firm on what was otherwise a successful, i.e. premium paying, corporate project. In thinking about the issue, I realize I may be veering off into paranoia, but I assure myself that as long as I do not discuss the issue with anybody else at the firm, it is probably my survival instincts kicking in again.

The MID-LEVEL LITIGATION PARTNER drops by.

"I have a client meeting. Very hot new deal. Like you to come along for lunch."

I mumble ascent.

After work, I drive to the MID-LEVEL LITIGATION PARTNER's house. He has a split level in Brentwood up in the hills. He's clearly doing all right.

I park discretely on the street next to a lime green van probably owned by some illegal gardener and we get into his 911 and drive to Mr. Chow's in Beverly Hills. The son of a bitch finds a parking space at a meter right in front of the restaurant, which I am sure is a first in the entire history of Beverly Hills.

"Go in and find our table," he instructs.

The hostess is breathtaking. Straight blond hair down to her butt crack, which is almost visible given the gauzy nature of the little A Line

Shift she is wearing. Piercing blue eyes. Lots of eyeliner. Mascara. She looks at me. I see her slightly trembling.

"That's a really nice car," she says.

At that moment, the MID-LEVEL LITIGATION PARTNER makes his appearance.

"That's his car," I say. I point.

The hostess makes direct eye contact with the MID-LEVEL LITIGATION PARTNER. She starts trembling again.

"That's a really nice car," she says.

The days of the cobalt blue Rabbit are numbered.

The client never shows. While we wait, the MID-LEVEL LITIGATION PARTNER makes small talk about how he had to import his speedometer from Germany because the export version on the Porsche only goes up to 120 mph. I try to remain polite and drink only small sips of very expensive white wine. The MID-LEVEL LITIGATION PARTNER hails from one of the vast stretches of America I have only flown over. After a tour at a land grant college, he polished off his resume at the Harvard of the Harbor freeway, as USC is locally known. He is now ruling the roost in LA.

I get to bed early. I lie awake for a while and reflect that there is real opportunity out West. The Pet Shop Boys have it all figured out.

DINNER AND DESERT

Monday. I am back with the CCH Tax Reporter on the 27th floor of the Arco Towers. Some subsidiary merger thing. I can't find the right code section. Steve comes in.

"So, I hear you are going out with Lonnie on Saturday," Steve says.

"She is a very nice girl," I say in my best preppy affected voice.

"I think she's hot," Steve says. Steve is too preppy to sound prurient, but I appreciate the attempt to relate to me on some baser level than the tax code. The guy hasn't even taken off his suit jacket.

"Gloria says that she really likes you," Steve says.

"Well, please thank Gloria for the introduction," I say.

Obligatory Wednesday telephone call to Lonnie.

"How you doing, honey?" she says.

"Great," I say. "Looking forward to Saturday. Been busy at work," I say.

Lonnie wants to meet at a steak house in Santa Monica named after Ben somebody. He is probably a friend of John Wayne. I find it without too much trouble. Parking is another story. They have way too many cars out here. Lonnie has made reservations (under my name). I like that. Lonnie comes bouncing in late, talking and waving her arms. A perpetual motion machine. I see that she has reversed her color scheme. She now has on a very pink, very low-cut top and a very short black skirt. She is wearing very high heels. They are both pink and black. Thematic unity.

"How you doing, honey?" Lonnie says.

"Good, it's nice to be with you again," I say. Another Stanford seduction line. As he says, if they have already done it once, it makes it a no brainer to do it again. I have been pretty much told in advance that Lonnie is looking for action. In Lonnie's case my idiot seduction line actually seems to work. She puts her hand on mine.

"You look nice, honey," says Lonnie. She giggles.

The waitress arrives at the table. She has the same helmet hair as the one at Mr. Blitstein's coffee shop in the valley. I start wondering if there is an LA rule that all waitresses have to have their hair done in the same salon. It must be in the Valley.

"You made up your minds?" says the helmet hair.

"I'll have a baked potato and a Caesar salad," blurts out Lonnie.

"OK, hun," says the helmet. "Anything to drink?"

"Diet Coke," says Lonnie. "With lemon."

"I would like a vodka martini straight up and the New York strip medium rare," I say. I realize I am being way too transparent about my priorities.

"Right away," says the helmet hair. She is thinking big drinker, big tab, and big tip. The inescapable logic of the hospitality industry.

Thankfully, the vodka martini arrives in a moment. After a few sips, I feel I am mentally prepared for some conversation with Lonnie. I figure I will stick to basic themes.

"So what happens after you graduate?" I ask.

Lonnie looks puzzled. Then she smiles. There seems to be some comprehension.

"I want to fly with the airlines," she says.

I process this. She comes from San Diego. Does she want to be a pilot or an astronaut? She has no engineering skills. I think Gloria told me she majored in psychology. I finally get it.

"You're kidding," I say. "You don't need to go to college to be an airline stewardess."

I am immediately angry at myself. After all Richard is not here for career counseling. They have someone who does that at UCLA. Richard is here to get laid.

"It's kind of a fantasy," Lonnie says. She giggles. "I was in this bar once and there were all these really good looking girls and they wanted to know who did I fly for. Don't you think I could fly for the airlines?"

Lonnie then cocks her head.

"Can I serve you?" she says. Lonnie giggles some more.

I am much less angry at myself.

"It's been a long day and I could really use some service," I say. I smile.

The helmet comes back to see about dessert, but Lonnie's restaurant repertoire is apparently limited to exactly what she ordered.

"Are you going to come home and have a drink with me?" Lonnie asks.

"Of course, darling," I say. "I'm going to let you practice for your first class passengers."

The thought seems to excite Lonnie. The helmet hair is happy with her tip. I walk Lonnie to her to her car. It is a white Ford Pinto. It looks like it is manufactured in one of the model years where it had the exploding gas tank. I don't comment. Lonnie hauls a key chain out of her pocketbook that has more keys on it than the super of 180 unit building in the Bronx. I follow her in the cobalt blue Rabbit down Santa Monica Boulevard to a three-story apartment building that looks like every other three-story apartment building on the block.

I sit on the couch. Everything is LA standard issue. Dimmer switches on the lights. Sliding glass doors. Wall to wall carpet. Medium shag. A few Carol King albums. Lonnie lights a candle. I discreetly go and pee. Every towel in the bathroom is either black or pink. I sense the same recurring theme. Lonnie returns from the kitchen with a tumbler filed with vodka and one ice cube.

"Here is your drink, Sir," she says. I notice her lip gloss has been refreshed.

Lonnie sits down next to me and her skirt hikes up to the reinforcement line on her pantyhose.

"What else is on the menu?" I ask.

Apparently this is all the "fly me" role playing that Lonnie can manage. She covers my mouth with hers and inserts her tongue down my throat. She is now unbuttoning my shirt. My tie is still on. Her skirt is hiked up over her crotch and she is moaning and dry humping my leg. After what seems an eternity, I pry loose enough from Lonnie's lip lock so that I can reach my tumbler of vodka and have a few gulps. Lonnie, apparently drawn into the conflict between a man, his women and his bottle, drops to her knees and starts tugging at my zipper.

"I want to kiss it, honey," she says.

I take another gulp of vodka. The development is not unwelcome and I am reflecting about what they put in the water in Los Angeles that makes women swallow semen on a first date. Now, Lonnie has my suit pants down around my ankles and is licking my member, which is responding nicely to all of the attention. I close my eyes. *No. This is a bad idea.* I feel this syrupy liquid dribbling down from the head of my penis. I open my eyes. Lonnie has ripped open a single serve packet of honey (organic no less) and is using her fingers to cover my whole organ with this stuff.

"What are you doing, Lonnie?" I say. I'm trying not to sound alarmed.

"I'm having desert," Lonnie says. "I just love the taste of honey."

I decide that I better postpone any reaction until I can have a conversation with Stanford. I am dealing with forces beyond control. I finish my tumbler of vodka while Lonnie has dessert. I manage to maintain an erection despite the loud slurping noises. Lonnie apparently views fellatio as a culinary, as well as a sexual, experience.

When I am feeling a little less sticky, Lonnie suggests that we continue in the bedroom. I follow. The sheets are black and the pillows pink. Why I am not surprised? She straddles me and starts moving methodically. Periods of loud moaning are punctuated by occasional eye contact followed by an immediate giggle. My unusual passivity is inspired by self-preservation. I don't know how much time Lonnie spends in the gym, but it is pretty clear that she could bench press me if she put her mind to it. Besides being on the bottom stops everything from spinning around. Eventually Lonnie collapses on top of me and stops moving. She continues to breathe heavily. I fall asleep.

The next morning, I wake up Lonnie to give her a kiss. When I pull onto Santa Monica Boulevard, I find my favorite business suit is stuck to my favorite underwear and they are both stuck to the driver's seat of my cobalt blue Rabbit. When I get back to the Marina, I put the whole mess in a plastic bag and find a dumpster. I can't even begin to think what I would tell the nice Asian girl at the dry cleaners on Via Marina. I spend the rest of the day showering and refinishing furniture.

Sunday morning the phone rings. The digital alarm clock reads 9:00 am. I'm thinking, doesn't anybody sleep in on Sunday in this town? I reach towards the phone, vaguely wondering about what's in the style section in the New York Times.

"Hi, honey. I'm so excited," Lonnie says, "K-Earth is playing the sixties."

Lonnie convinces me to pick her up in front of her apartment and have breakfast. She waits on the curb. Gloria is still asleep. Lonnie is wearing pink short shorts, a black halter top, and black high heels. We drive to the Good Earth restaurant in Westwood. Lonnie turns the radio to K-Earth and sings along. I am philosophical. It could be Mariachi music. We sit at a four top. Lonnie orders nine grain pancakes. I couldn't name nine grains if it were the $64,000 question on a game show. When Lonnie excuses herself to go to the bathroom, I have a flash of inspiration. I put her giant handbag next to me and inventory the contents. Thank God. Nothing causes alarm. There is a lot of gum, breath mints, the gigantic key chain, a few crumpled dollar bills, and a plastic package of honey. No hot sauce.

We end up back in my apartment in the Marina. Lonnie is amorous the minute we get inside the door. I discover that by mounting her from behind and putting all my weight on the small of her back I can control her pelvic thrusting and climax. Pulling her hair helps as well. She doesn't seem to mind. There is still lot's of moaning, but no eye contact and no giggles.

At 6:00 pm, I send Lonnie back to Westwood in a cab. I have a major week coming up.

REDEYE

It seems like a normal Monday except that THE HEAD OF THE TAX DEPARTMENT is waiting for me in my office.

I have to admit that he looks like a tax lawyer. THE HEAD OF THE TAX DEPARTMENT has grey hair. He wears wire rimmed glasses. He has a very serious, but tentative manner.

"I've got a plum assignment for you, Richard. You are going to be the Tax Department's representative for a usury opinion on an important preferred stock deal."

He tosses a fat prospectus on my desk.

"This will be a very helpful precedent for you."

"Thank you, sir."

I read carefully. I rapidly come to the conclusion that my work on this transaction could be replaced by a photocopy machine. The "helpful precedent" is the cookie and I am to act as the cookie cutter. I ask around the department and the scam is pretty obvious. California, in its zeal to protect poor consumers from the ravages of East Coast capitalists, have very strict rules to protect its citizens from excessive interest – or what is called "usury." However, the zeal of the legislature has left ambiguities and some kinds of stock can literally be read within the scope of the prohibition.

The solution is sheer genius – if you are a greedy California lawyer. All you have to do is remove the transaction from the harsh California sunshine and have it negotiated and consummated in some other state. Then you write a "reasoned" opinion, which is code for an opinion with so many qualifications that it really is not an opinion at all, to the effect that California law does not apply. At closing you present a bill for $17,595. An associate does all the work and the firm realizes a very fat profit.

Of course, "somewhere else" is Manhattan because it is convenient for the investment bank raising the money. Since my whereabouts are where the transaction "is", my life becomes a living hell.

On Tuesday, I leave the office at 8:00 pm and head not for home, but for LAX. I take the 10:00 pm flight to JFK, have three vodkas in a row in an attempt to gain a few hours of sleep, and arrive at 6:30 am. I check into the Holiday Inn outside of La Guardia, long enough to shower, shave, and put on a clean shirt. I make it down to Wall Street for a 9:00 am meeting. I make the 7:00 pm flight back to LAX, and with the aid of a few more shots of vodka, I am asleep by 1:00 am. The next day I am back in the office – after all, I do have other clients. This schedule is to repeat itself until I collapse or the deal is closed.

The Redeye is really not part of Los Angeles. It is a piece of New York and functions by New York and not LA rules. From the second you are on the plane you are surrounded by individuals scanning every empty seat, which might permit them to lie down for the next six hours and actually get some sleep. The second the door to the plane is closed, the swiftest among the seat scanners literally hurl themselves at these spaces and secure them with pillows or briefcases. They buckle their seat belts knowingly on top of their blankets and fall into a heavy barbiturate induced sleep.

On the fifth Tuesday, the plane is packed and even the empty seat scanners have given up hope. I am sitting next to a rather swarthy gentleman. After the pilot announces we have reached cruising altitude, he takes out what appears to be a woman's contact case filled with white powder. He begins snorting it though a short silver straw. His entire body begins twitching and then he goes absolutely still.

I walk down the aisle and tell the stewardess that my fellow passenger may be in some kind of health related distress.

"Did he threaten your life?" she asks.

"No."

"The FAA says there is nothing I can do about it."

I make a resolution to stay away from all future "plum assignments."

THANK YOU FOR CALLING FRED ALLEN

I had implemented all three parts of Stanford Blitstein's three-part program of Southern Californian cultural integration. I had my cobalt blue metallic wheels, my stereo with its giant throbbing speakers, and my girlfriend who could be on a poster for the Cybex exercise machine company. I am still not happy. Something is missing. Lonnie had called me last night and told me that she and Gloria were going to serve dinner to Steve and I while wearing French maid's costumes. Of course, she had to special order hers because it only came in black and she wanted pink. Normally, the thought of Lonnie prancing around in a maid's costume, pleading to be of service, would have been an enormously hard on provoking idea, but the pink special order part somehow dampened the excitement. I called Stanford in Boston.

"So what's the problem?" he asked.

"It's not fun anymore," I say. "I am worried Lonnie is going to cover my penis in hot sauce."

"Of course, it's not. You're just starting to get into it. Now you've got to push the envelope to make it fun," Stanford says.

He really stresses the *"into it"* part.

"You need to trade up."

"Trade up," I say without real understanding.

"The Rabbit is only three months old."

"How old is Lonnie?" he asks

"22," I say.

"Get a younger one."

"You think younger is going to be better?" I ask.

"Always," Stanford says. "Think about a women uncorrupted by the materialism of Southern California. A woman that you can mold into what you want her to be. A woman who will be dazzled with your age and experience. A woman that you can train to please you."

I am clearly not relating to this whole "Of Human Bondage" thing.

"Why don't you come visit?" I ask.

"I will. I will," Stanford says. Stanford sounds less than convincing.

"I have got to finish up this research paper I am working on with another graduate student."

"Is she from Eastern Europe?" I ask.

"How did you know?" Stanford says. He sounded genuinely surprised.

I walk on the docks of the Marina, look at the boats and reflect a good bit on my conversation with Stanford. He seems unaffected by attacks of self doubt; he certainly gets laid on a regular basis, although I don't understand his current preoccupation with the babes from the Eastern Bloc. Maybe it is the high cheekbones.

It just so happens that David, the wimp from law school, calls me and invites me to a party in Beverly Hills. David is the little fuck that set me up with the babes in the track shorts at the UCLA law library in an effort to make me fail the bar. He has a younger sister who is just starting UCLA. That is interesting by itself, if only the possibility of fucking her for revenge. I call back and say yes. I don't care what Stanford says about trading up, I am not going to start running after high school chicks in the Pacific Palisades, even if they are eighteen and street legal.

Saturday night. The house in question is in the flats of Beverly Hills – a triumph of zip code over geography. It is also a masterpiece of 1960s sputnik inspired décor, brought up to date by the inclusion of chocolate sectional furniture. Loud music. I have never known anybody named "Sharona," but they keep yelling her name. David's sister is short, squat, red headed and unfuckable. I plop down on the sofa next to a girl with the frizziest hair I have ever seen. She is sitting with legs crossed and wearing a white mini and what appears to be a pair of two toned men's wing tips. The price tag is still on the bottom of the right one.

"Did you really pay 125 dollars for those shoes?" I ask.

"*Ohmagod*, this is sooo embarrassing," Ms. Frizzy says.

"I'm Richard," I say.

"Sally Green."

"You've got an English accent," I say

"My mum's English."

"So you want to go outside and talk? It's too loud in here. Who is Sharona?"

Sally laughs. I like Sally. She laughs at my jokes and lives in the Valley. Her father is an accountant. Her mother is a real estate broker of sorts. Her mother's brother is in the theater. Other than the 125 dollar shoes, which she bought at a store where her sister works, there is nothing pretentious about her. She lives at home. She is just nineteen. She is a freshman at UCLA and she is coming over for dinner.

Obligatory Wednesday telephone call.

"Thank you for calling Fred Allen," says a voice on the other end of the line. I recheck the phone number. Even a tax lawyer can transpose a digit.

"Is this the Green residence?"

"Yes," says the same voice.

"This is Richard. I would like to talk to Sally."

"Uh huh," says the same voice.

"Hi," says Sally.

"What's with 'thank you for calling Fred Allen?'"

"Oonah just came home from work and she doesn't do well with transitions."

"Pasta, OK?" I am thinking about Lonnie and her inability to eat anything but baked potatoes, Caesar salad and honey covered penises.

"Sure."

I drive to the valley and pick up Sally. She lives in one of the Canyons. A good sign, I think. Geography has triumphed over zip code. Sally is definitely dressed to date. Short pleated skirt, tight white top and red come fuck me shoes.

I go inside and meet her parents. She has inherited her mother's very large breasts. Her father is gray and originally from Brooklyn. I ask them where they met. They both seemed to like the question. I tune out a little while they answer. It was some kind of a Zionist social. I talk a little tax with Daddy. He seems about ten years older than his wife. Things are looking good.

Sally likes my apartment. We look at the boats. I think I will never be able to afford one of these. I don't know what Sally is thinking. Pasta is ok. I put on some Miles Davis. Bass up. The Crazy Eddy speakers start to throb. We settle on the couch. Sally talks about her love of Italy. She has never been. Must be the mother. Most of the Brits have this Italian thing. It comes from living in the damp most of the year. England is a primitive country. You have to pay for heat by the hour by shoving giant coins with anchors on them into a meter. English hooker heating. Can't blame the mother. Sally's breasts are huge. I keep getting my mouth close to hers and she makes the first move. Hey, 19. Not bad, I'm thinking. I'm running my hands up her thighs. No resistance. Her panties are wet. Stanford is right. Younger is better. Much better. My hand moves under her panties. Really wet. Little moans. This is better than hand crushing Cybexated thighs of Lonnie. Wait a second. A glance downward indicates that my right hand is red. I did chicken with the pasta and a white wine sauce. No marina. Then my blood starved brain finally processes all of the data. *Sally is having her period. She is having her period on my suede couch.* The same couch that my mother bought me at Bloomingdales. My physical reaction is obvious. Sally pulls back.

I am relieved. I don't have to dump the suede couch in East LA and resort to Corinthian leather. Sally unzips the cushion, asks for a plastic bag and tells me that she knows the best dry cleaner in the Valley. In fact, she tells me that her sister at Fred Allen has had similar problems with suede skirts and irritable models. I feel much better. Younger is better. I'm repeating it like a mantra. I trust Stanford. I drive Sally home. It's 11:00 in the evening. Mum and Daddy are very relieved to see me. We are holding hands. I have a cup of tea with Daddy and talk some more tax. I kiss Sally good night. Mum still seems to approve. I inspect the passenger seat on the Rabbit before I drive back. All is still good.

I DON'T KNOW WHO YOU WERE
FUCKING LAST NIGHT,
BUT IT WASN'T ME

I took off Friday afternoon — the whole afternoon. Unusual for me. It must be the prospect of intercourse with a 19 year old. Is this what Stanford meant by pushing the envelope? I meet Sally in a rundown café in Venice. Another tight top. This one is sort of a light pink. Big sunglasses. Must be the Italian influence. She seems to have lost the two tone shoes. The conversation is more focused on the weekend.

"Is Sunday night OK?" I say.

"Sure."

"I'm talking about a sleep over. Is your Mom OK with this?"

"Sure."

"I want to do this fantasy thing."

"OK," Sally says.

I get a "this guy wants me to wear rubber diapers" reaction. After all her mother is English. She undoubtedly has an uncle in London she didn't mention who is incapable of maintaining an erection without wearing a full latex body suit.

"Frilly underwear, "I say. "You know the stuff the models wear in Penthouse?"

"OK." She sounds positively reassured.

I hand her a picture I tore out of the last issue. Sally inspects it closely.

I sense this great deal of relief. This is clearly something she can work out with sister Oonah, who, after all, is in the fashion world. She doesn't have to consult with any of her father's accounting clients who are in the raw materials business. We kiss and I get on the freeway.

I reflect on the 5th Street on-ramp that if I tried this stunt in New Jersey my mother would get a call from my date's mother's therapist. I get back to Flower Street just in time for rush hour to start. No point sitting on the Santa Monica Freeway. The alternative is crazed lane changing locals on Olympic Boulevard. Neither of these alternatives seems very pleasant. However, it's Friday night and the regulars are already in the bar. Young lawyers don't have to buy drinks. There is seemingly an inexhaustible number of see-through cocktails with the final bar tab being picked up by the most senior guy there. I sense it isn't the guilt from how much money he is making off of exploiting us, but I am sure he still chits the entire bill to associate relations. After two see-through cocktails I am starting to feel pretty good. I eat enough nuts to call it dinner. THE SENIOR PARTNER ORIGINALLY FROM KANSAS with the movie star tan is complaining that no one can figure out how to bail out a real estate partnership without recognizing cancellation of indebtedness income. The three other associates at my table look on attentively. The cocktail waitress who has slept with at least half of the lawyers in my class brings another round.

"You do a holding company," I say. I am amazed the Internal Revenue Code still triumphs over the Demon Rum.

"It's a partnership," he says. I detect just a little too much patronizing in his voice.

"Not a corporate holding company," I say. "I'm talking about a partnership that would act like a holding company and holds all of the equity in the partnership you are trying to recap."

I see Kansas's brain chugging through the concept. Little too much of the sauce. Of course he can't digest it completely. He turns to one of the young tax partners who nods at him affirmatively.

He still reflects. Probably trying to calculate out how many cocktails his tax guy has had.

"Richard, you come see me first thing Monday."

"Yes, Sir."

I couldn't exit immediately. I continued to participate in the inane conversation with my associate companions about who is really screwing the receptionist on the 26th floor for another fifteen minutes. I leave the bar at exactly 6:50 pm. I am feeling better than pretty good. I just picked up a new deal and THE SENIOR PARTNER ORIGINALLY FROM KANSAS seems to feel that I am a valuable addition to the team. Since most of the value is expropriated by him, he is feeling good as well. I am feeling even better about doing the nineteen-year-old Penthouse photo shoot on Sunday. The timing of my exit is based upon experience. If I get on the Santa Monica freeway at 6:50 pm, it doesn't matter that I am just on the verge of an alcohol induced stupor. All I have to do is drive in a straight line at 27 miles per hour for 45 minutes. That is plenty of time to sober up. I don't have to obey red lights or make complicated turns until I get to the Marina.

At the apartment, there is mail in my box. It's a post card of some babe with huge breasts in a demi bikini. "Wish you were here. XXXXX." It is from Julie of Orange County. Julie seems like another era. Spandex and silicon has nothing on a nineteen-year-old dressed like a Victorian call girl who got lost in a London alley on her way to a meeting with Dr. Jekyll. Wielding the tax code like a rapier among powerful drunks who control my future has made me tired. I crawl into bed and fall quickly asleep. No dreams that night. I am living them.

Saturday night - meaning date night. It does not go well. For some reason the thought of a nineteen-year-old dressed like a Penthouse Pet is a little overwhelming and I start doing hits on the bong I hide next to the plunger under the sink in the galley kitchen at 4:00 pm. I am more than a little bleary when Sally shows up at 6:00 pm. Of course, she is nervous and disappears in the bathroom to do wardrobe for an hour, which is even worse, because it gives me the opportunity to take a few more hits off the bong hidden behind the plunger.   Sally appears - an image of nineteen-year-old loveliness wearing pink garters, a lacey black push-up bra, and pink lip gloss. I am overcome with lust. Instead of being reassuring, a sentiment that these girls all need from their director before they enter stage right, I simply lead her to the bedroom, thrust vigorously until I climax and promptly pass out.

I wake up to the smell of coffee. Sally is now wearing one of my white tee shirts hands me a mug. I am coming back to life.

"Very thoughtful. Thank you," I say.

"I don't know who you thought that you were fucking last night, but it wasn't me," Sally says.

TINY BUBLES

I am deeply disturbed by the "I don't know who you thought were fucking last night, but it wasn't me" comment. Sally has somehow hit a raw nerve. I am beginning to question whether Los Angeles is really a sort of wild life preserve for sexual game. Nineteen-year-olds are not supposed to insult you, much less insult you in a way that makes you feel like you are living a wasted and wanton life. I am feeling doubt and I decide to do what I always do while confronting moral issues that could have a moral dimension.

I call Blitstein.

He is in a rather expansive mood.

"Hot date?"

"I met this woman from Siberia," Blitstein said.

"She has perfect cheek bones," I said.

"How did you know that?"

"I saw it on this Discovery Channel."

Actually, I did read a book at the Harvard Library on racial typology written in 1941 by the Hermann Goering, chair of Volks Anthropology at the University of Tuebingen, but I did not want to get into another lecture series with Blitstein.

"I am following your program and I am becoming guilt ridden," I say.

"Patience, Lad."

"What do you mean, patience?"

"Liquor."

"You are lecturing *me* about the virtues of alcohol abuse?"

"No, I mean it. Alcohol unleashes the inner demon. It strips off that thin veneer of civilization. And you have the advantage. Her liver works better than yours."

"You are just getting yourself warmed up for the Siberian slut," I say.

I need to follow a clear mandate, and there is no clearer mandate than the pronouncements of Blitstein.

I go to the sleazy liquor store on Venice Boulevard. What are they drinking at the entry level these days? No more seven and seven. Probably something you mix with Coke.

The clerk behind the counter is even sleazier than the store and I soon fall out of the high ball mood. I end up buying two very expensive bottles of champagne in a flowered bottle – rose. Perfect. The clerk is very approving, probably the largest sale he has had in a month. When he smiles, I can see at least one missing tooth.

"A nice champagne," he says. "It has tiny bubbles."

"Thanks," I say.

I notice there is not much change for two hundred.

Sally shows up later looking at least twenty-four. She has on a black cocktail dress where you can see the sides of her boobs. I abstain from taking any mind expanding drugs and I am very solicitous.

I put a little Vivaldi on the stereo, drape the flowered bottle with a clean kitchen towel (the only one I have), and open the bottle, observing with great satisfaction the little wisp of champagne smoke forming at the top of the bottle.

For some reason, I start lecturing Sally about class conflict in medieval Japanese society. This is a topic that had gotten me an "A" in a literature in translation course where I had not even done the required reading, but I did have extensive discussions with the Professor about his sex fantasies about all of the women in the class. Thank God, it had been a small class, because he tended to like women with chronic coughs who should have been reading novels in the solarium at a sanatorium in Switzerland instead of taking college courses in the state of Massachusetts.

Sally is making a lot of eye contact. I think this whole Marxist rant is successfully obscuring the fact that, in reality, I am more of a capitalist tool than Forbes magazine.

While I am lecturing, Sally is tossing back pink champagne. She is getting visibly amorous. She giggles. Sally is now losing interest in narrative regarding about how many petticoats women wore in feudal Japanese society. She is staring at my crotch.

"I want to suck on it," she says.

I notice that the pink liquid no longer fills the bottle with my only clean hand towel draped over it.

"You need to plead to suck it," I say. I am vaguely annoyed that my lecture on the importance of petticoats in sexual arousal in feudalism is being interrupted.

Sally is beyond blushing. She is very horny.

"Please, please may I suck it?" she says.

This is progress, I think. The thin veneer of civilization is being stripped away just like the polyurethane on a table top in an LA coffee shop. I am reflecting on intonation of Sally's second please.

I get up. Sally has her eyes closed and is pursing her lips.

The opening of the second bottle does not go as well. The cork explodes and leaves a dent on the spray-on acoustic ceiling of my apartment.

"Look, it's coming," Sally says.

She is all done with pleading. Her hands are in my crotch and she is tugging at my zipper. Next my pants are around my ankles and Sally is demonstrating that she may be nineteen, but she has seen more than one porno.

This time she leads me to the bedroom. She straddles me facing the mirrored wall and I get a great view of her ass bouncing up and down while she makes meaningful eye contact with me in the mirror. Sally slams down hard on my cock and starts grinding to the point where I want to explode and then she stops. More positions, more pink champagne, and finally collapse.

The next morning is a workday. I manage to shower, find a clean shirt and my car keys. Sally is breathing heavily and I decide to let her sleep in.

Unfortunately, I have a pre-closing that morning. I am in the process of counting stock certificates when I hear a page.

I answer the phone. The operator tells me it is an emergency call.

"This is Mrs. Green, Sally's mother," the voice on the other end says.

"Yes, Mrs. Green," I say.

There is something about the vague panic in my voice and, in a matter of seconds, the other four associates in the conference room are looking intently at me.

"Sally didn't come home last night," says Mrs. Green.

"That is absolutely the case. I thought everything had been precleared with you," I say. I am trying desperately to sound like I am talking to a client.

"I thought she might have spent the night with you," says Mrs. Green.

"That is absolutely the case," I say.

"Then, you won't have a problem with me going over to your apartment and picking her up," Mrs. Green says.

"Absolutely, no problem."

I am trying desperately to remember if I left anything illegal in plain view in the apartment. I turn to the other four associates who are still staring intently.

"Clients are such a pain," I say.

My audience goes back to work.

THE PERTIKEN DIET

Next day, I am sitting at my desk.

I decide if it is best if I give Sally a couple of days off. I am still pissed about her mother calling me at work. Then again, it's just another California rule. Overly protective mothers seem to make for sexually available daughters.

Shelia O'Brien calls.

"How are you?"

"I am in Santa Monica."

"I asked how are you, not where are you," I say.

Sheila is a law school classmate. She laughs.

"I thought you did tax, not litigation. Please don't take my deposition. I'm OK," she says. "My mother is not. She is drying out. We are both at the Pertiken foundation in Santa Monica. They are making me crazy. How about dinner?"

Sheila was a law school flame. The flame that burns twice as brightly burns half as long. Our relationship flamed out in about two weeks. I spent another couple of months driving her 1965 vintage MG while she recovered from a nervous break down following the break up with her long term boyfriend. Sex with me turned out to be a final acting out in the last chapter of that relationship. It was a much better deal than being her boyfriend.

Sheila is OK. She is very blond and very boyish – no boobs, no frilly panties and no prom dresses. I remember spending a lot of time mounting her from behind.

Well, there is Sheila standing at the massive iron gate which is the entrance to the Pertiken Foundation. She is wearing a white tank top and skirt with pink orchids on it. She looks, as she generally did, as if she has just gotten out of bed.

I hand her my cigarette and she inhales it like it a joint.

"It is horrible in there," Sheila says. "No meat, no booze, no cheese. They give you herbal tea six times a day. It is supposed to clean you out."

Sheila spits out the word herbal like it is some kind of poison.

"So, what in God's name are you doing in there?"

"My Dad says he is going to divorce my mother if she doesn't stop drinking and I am here to give her moral support."

"Steak for dinner?"

"Absolutely," she says.

I drive to Ben Benson's in Santa Monica. I realize I have not been there since my encounter with Lonnie who ate nothing but baked potatoes, Caesar salad, and honey coated penises. I have a vague feeling of concern when I wonder whether her Pinto has exploded yet.

The helmet headed blond waitress seems to remember me. I am drinking martinis. Sheila doesn't even bother with Vermouth - she is on her third straight Vodka. Now, Sheila is eating chunks of red meat and smoking in between chomps.

"I feel better," she says.

"You are making me dizzy," I say. "My Dad was into Pertiken for a while after he had a heart attack. At first he kept talking about how cheese looked in your arteries exactly the same way it looked on your plate. It got to be a real drag. Then, he decided that what was the point of living another year or two if you couldn't have a corned beef sandwich."

"Exactly. These Pertiken people are horrible people. They take all meaning away from life," Sheila says.

She looks at her watch.

"I have to be back in 45 minutes. There is a curfew."

I dutifully drive Shelia back to the Pertiken foundation. Sheila is quiet, evidently lost in thought and sucking on a breath mint. I realize she is calculating how she can get by the nurse without the discovery of her remarkable consumption of contraband in the last three hours.

"What happened to us?" she asks.

"You sort of just left," I say.

"It must have been a bad time for me."

Sheila straddles me on the driver's seat and kisses me full on the mouth. She tastes like wintergreen. Both her mouth and her pussy are very wet. I discretely pull out my member and pull her panties to the side. She rocks back and forth and it doesn't take long for both of us to climax – almost at the same time. In another moment she is gone.

I guess she got to quota and was now ready to face the rest of the week.

LESS THAN VIVID PRODUCTIONS

Porno has got to be the second biggest industry in LA after making electronic weapons of mass destruction. Having grown up in Hackensack, New Jersey, I don't know that for sure, but I guess I could have researched the point.

The ASSIGNING PARTNER is running out of tax assignments. He calls me into the office and mumbles something about "spreading the wealth." Spreading the shit is more like it. It seems that firm management is going to broaden my experience and expose me to its entertainment law practice. The "fact pattern" – a phrase we loved to use in law school – is pretty simple. The firm represents a Mexican beer distributor. It has been running commercials in Mexico City for years where Southern California girls with huge breasts and tiny bathing suits run on the beach, play volleyball and then drink their beer from long neck bottles with great gusto and exaggerated smacking noises. Subtlety is not part of Spanish language television advertising. Now somebody is piping Mexican television into Los Angeles on some cable channel. The girls with the tiny bathing suits who are flipping channels late at night want to know when they are getting their residual checks. Some of them can even swear in Spanish and have called the beer distributor. Time for Los Abbigados de Los Angeles to solve the problem.

I am equipped with a list of names, a clipboard, a release form and checks that have "Not valid for more than $500" stamped on them. None of these girls are at home. They all live in seedy apartment buildings on cross streets varying distances from Ventura Boulevard. I leave my card with a note on the top that says I want to talk to them about residuals. This produces results.

"Richard," says the telephone. "This is Loretta Moan."

"Yes, Loretta." I think this girl has got a very breathy voice.

"Can you meet me in Northridge tomorrow on location?"

"Sure," I say. "Give me the address."

The location is yet another split level in the San Fernando Valley with a pool. I could be anywhere in the valley. There are two panel trucks parked outside. They are doing renovations, I think.

The front door is slightly ajar. I open it. They are not doing renovations. There is a five man film crew. Klieg lights. Reflecting screens. A couple copulating on the couch. Somebody motions me to be quiet. I look just a little out of place with a muted red paisley tie and a Brooks Brothers suit. The other males are wearing very open rayon shirts with gold chains. The actress is wearing nothing but a thigh high pair of black patent leather boots. A very large member is being thrust in and out of the vaginal opening that appears at the top of the boots. Voyeurism is better than tax research. I lean up against a wall and prepare to watch. I don't get much of a chance to watch.

"Cut," yells the guy with the hairiest chest, the most open shirt and the most gold chains. He turns towards me.

"What the fuck do you want?" Obviously elevated testosterone levels.

"I am Richard Parker. I'm here to see Ms. Moan. I have an appointment."

Ms. Moan turns out to be the patent leather lust object on the couch. Somebody has handed her a towel. She wipes off most of her co-actor's bodily fluids and approaches me. Her breasts do not move when she walks. The fact she can even walk in the leather thigh highs is a remarkable feat in itself, I think.

"How much?"

I have to say that I admire directness in a porno star.

"I am authorized on behalf of my client to pay you $500 for a release of your residual rights in all of your roles in its commercials."

Ms. Moan looks at me quizzically. I observe her staring at my tie like it is a fossil from the late Cro-Magnon period in the museum of natural history. I am trying very hard not to stare at her gigantic breasts. They must be twice the size of Sally's. I remember reading that Dolly Parton had back problems. I fear this woman is going to need a spinal implant.

"500 bucks now and no residual checks," Ms. Moan says.

"Exactly," I say. "You are extremely perceptive, Ms. Moan."

I produce the clipboard with the release. Ms. Moan signs. I smile. I hand her a check stamped prominently with "no value over $500". I notice that the leading man is being fellated by another woman in normal street clothes and glasses.

"Enough fluff," says Mr. Multiple Gold Chain. "Take".

Ms. Moan walks back to the couch. I noticed her ass does move when she walks. I feel better about the porno industry. She leans over the couch with her naked ass in the air, the klieg lights come back on and I get out and into the cobalt metallic blue Rabbit.

It turns out that Ms. Moan has a lot of friends in the industry. The next day at the office I have about ten messages from other adult film actresses. I have learned from my experience with Ms. Moan.

I am waiting in a coffee shop for Friend of Ms. Moan No. 1 to show up.

Two guys with gold chains in the booth behind me are having an animated conversation.

"So where were you? You missed the party," says El Chaino No. 1.

"I drove up to Camarillo State for the patient's art show," says El Chaino No. 2.

"You drove to a mental institution?" says El Chaino No. 1. He is obviously having some difficulty digesting this fact.

"Some of this patient stuff looks exactly like Samuel Bacon," says El Chaino No. 2. "I got three great oils for less than $50. It's very tortured stuff. The chicks in Brentwood love it."

Ms. Moan's friend shows up. She has the same Moan-like physique. She says even less. When she sees the check for $500 she signs the release immediately. I make more appointments and have many more meetings in coffee shops on Ventura Boulevard. Nobody else is buying art from mental patients. I give the secretary to the entertainment partner a very big stack of releases. I get very good reviews from the entertainment partner. He says I am an enterprising young man and will go far in the firm. I get a big bonus at Christmas.

DEEP SEA FISH BARBIE

Blitstein's sister is getting married.

I had met her exactly once before. It was at a bar in London. She was a platinum blond. She was attending NYU film school at the time. It is a degree, I thought, that guaranteed that at one point in her life she would be collecting unemployment. She smoked, a lot, and left abruptly to see her boyfriend. Blitstein says that he was in Israeli intelligence.

I call Blitstein in Boston.

"What's with the wedding invitation?"

"You have to come. There is nothing like a wedding to make women complete sexual animals. They sense the possibilities."

"You are exaggerating as usual."

"It is going to be a feeding frenzy."

The affair at the Beverly Wilshire is tasteful in an ostentatious *nouveau riche* kind of way. They have lots of flowers and Chinese chicken salad for lunch. I sit at a table of distant cousins. I am grateful to be singled out as a family friend. After all, I could be at the table with the concrete suppliers or the coach of the high school track team.

The young lady immediately next to me has very black hair, very white skin and very red lipstick. I kind of like the Adams Family look.

"So what do you do, Barbara?" I read the name off her little place card on the table.

"Barbie."

"Oh. So, what do you do, Barbie?"

"I am a student at Santa Monica."

I am afraid I look blank. I am trying desperately to remember what college is located in the People's Republic of Santa Monica. Maybe an institute for the study of folk art. Barbie-Leticia picks up immediately on my blankness.

"Santa Monica College."

"Oh." I am straining again to recover from an abysmal lack of knowledge of where the lumpenproletariat is educated.

"So you like have any favorite courses?"

"I have a course on oceanography."

"That's interesting."

"I just got this book on deep sea fish. They are weird."

Now, deep sea fish is not necessarily one of the burning interests of my life, but Barbie's red, red lips and the fluttering of her glued on eyelashes were starting to captivate me. I feel an erection stirring.

"I would really like to come over and see it. I mean the fish."

Barbie writes down her address on the back of the little place card and handed it to me.

"Tuesday at 6:00," says the red lips.

"Great," I say. I mean it.

I am late. Reading a Thomas Brothers map is not easy when you are in the fast lane on the Freeway. I get off on the wrong exit and have to take surface streets for miles. Barbie lives in one of those seedy apartment buildings in the Eastern reaches of Santa Monica. Rent control is not much of an incentive for repainting stucco.

I know I should bring something for Barbie, but I have no idea what. Flowers somehow do not seem appropriate for a seventeen-year-old student who probably has one pair of clean panties to her name. There is a toy store next to the supermarket. I buy a Ballroom Barbie doll. I ask the lady behind the counter to wrap it up with paper with red and yellow balloons on it. I don't want anyone walking around the neighborhood to think I am a child molester.

Barbie answers the door. She is wearing black leggings and a black top. No shoes.

Barbie has not been lying. I have been suppressing a feeling that the deep sea fish is a little like my collection of Japanese stamps, but, no, she has this big oversized volume filled with full color plates of the weirdest fish I had ever seen.

Barbie turned the pages methodically. Her upper lip curled in apparent concentration.

"This is my favorite."

The damn thing looks exactly like a penis.

"Nice."

Barbie seems to lose interest after the penis-deep-sea-fish.

"Let's see what you bought me."

Barbie slices through the balloons with a single long red finger nail. She looks at the package, slides out Ballroom Barbie and emits tiny oohs and ahhs.

"She's beautiful. Let's play."

Barbie pulls out Barbie's attached miniature comb and hairbrush and attends to Ballroom Barbie's elaborate coiffure. Both Barbies give me a long hungry look.

Ballroom Barbie is suddenly relegated to the coffee table top with the book filled with the pictures of penis-deep-sea-fish. The real Barbie drops to her knees, unzips my pants and gives me the best blow job I have had since I moved to Los Angeles. I guess she really liked her present.

AUGMENTATION

Barbie makes it pretty clear over the course of a couple of phone calls in the next few days that she has lost interest in both the deep-sea-fish-penis and mine. I figure that she has found some guy with a motorcycle.

On the other hand, the receptionist on the 26th floor has been casting long looks at me and making sighs after she murmurs "have a nice lunch" and "have a nice day." Having been cast off by Barbie and her limited attention span for deep-sea-fish and the human equivalent, I am finding myself more and more infatuated by the 26th floor receptionist. I discover that she has a little name plate on her desk that says "Georgette." I view this as a sign for a transition to get over the recent rejection of deep-sea-fish Barbie.

Keen observation is required. I smile a lot and say "hello" to Georgette during my trips to the offices of various senior corporate partners. I discover over the next few days that Georgette is fond of fuzzy Angora sweaters. Georgette has huge breasts, blond hair and very full, very pouty lips.

On Friday morning, I get into work early, say "hello" to Georgette, smile, get a very large cup of coffee and sit at my desk, resolving to take two days off from my continuing close study of the Internal Revenue Code. I open the pencil drawer. Inside is a little teddy bear with a heart shaped tag on which is written "You're cute, Georgette."

The parallels between this week and last are becoming overwhelming.

I dial zero.

"Reception 26."

"What about dinner tonight?"

Georgette sounds breathless.

"Yes."

"I need an address."

Georgette lives right off of Hollywood Boulevard. The hills tower above her bedroom like some unattainable height that she will never reach.

We have dinner at Musso & Frank's, which is sort of the end of the Hollywood Boulevard. We sit in the back in a booth. The prospect of being discovered by somebody from the firm is titillating, but remains unspoken between us. My career, needless to say, would not have been advanced by office rumors of me doing the 26th floor receptionist. Especially since her breasts were the subject of numerous conversations after a few cocktails at the Pub.

We return to the feet of the Hollywood hills. Georgette has a lot of Teddy Bears in her bedroom. Cuddles. Wet kisses. The smooth feel of Angora.

I slide my hand up her sweater looking for a clasp.

Georgette freezes up on me.

She looks at me. Blue eyes.

"I have scars from my operation."

I look blankly.

"I am augmented."

I am touched. I take off her bra slowly and deliberately. I kissed the scar where they moved her nipples to a more normal position on the massive mounds that were created by inserting two liter size silicon sacks. I try not to focus on the free will issue.

She seems relieved.

I spend the remainder of the evening fucking her doggie style. Georgette has a wonderful ass. It doesn't need to be augmented. We both seem happy about that position. No more sad stories or questions about malpractice.

The Teddy Bear stays in my pencil drawer. I sometimes look at it when a senior partner has the temerity to summon me to his office and question my judgment.

I FIRE MY LIFESTYLE CONSULTANT

Cary invites me to a party. He lives in Santa Monica. Right at the corner of Pacific Coast Highway.

The party consists of numerous women with spandex tops. Nobody seems particularly interested in me or available.

Stewart catches my attention. The spandex tops have gravitated to a couch where they are all piled upon each other. The spandex tops are engaged in elaborate grooming rituals while making conversation. It looks like what the monkeys do in the Bronx Zoo when they have lice. From the little snippets of conversation that I can hear, the major topics are what behaviors are required in order to not have men trade one in. Like cars, there are both performance and maintenance procedures.

Stewart is entertaining the males of the species. They are gathered in a circle of track shoes, denim and plastic bear cups. The sand is at their feet. The conversation is laid back, but with a heavy touch of testosterone.

"The babe is awesome," Stewart says. "She swallowed it on the first date."

Cary explains to me that Stewart lives in the Malibu beach colony. Stewart's apartment has less than 500 square feet and is located above a garage, but Stewart is quite vocal about his residential credentials.

Cary also explains to me that Stewart is the Chief Financial Officer of the Beverly Hills Oil Company. The sole asset of the Beverly Hills Oil Company consists of a stripper well in the basement of some office building off of Doheny. Visits to oil fields are made exclusively by Limo.

In other words, I grasp, Stewart is a consummate fraud. But this is the land of sunshine. I am not here to condemn. I am here to parody and to profit. If a lowly accountant can achieve this level of random oral gratification, the prognosis for an accomplished tax lawyer, such as me, is better than good.

I am inspired. The sand is at my feet.

"Stewart," I say. "I just moved here from the East Coast." I thought it better to drop the Hackensack thing. "I would like you to be my lifestyle consultant."

"Meaning?"

The tone is more quizzical than aloof.

"You need to advise me on what I need to do to be cool in Los Angeles."

"Sure. Cool," says Stewart.

Stewart pulls out his key chain. He's got a BMW. The key chain is a miniature track shoe.

"Wait a second, Stewart. Adidas' have three stripes," I say.

I see Stewart and his key chain at a party a few weeks later. One of the stripes had been carefully sliced off.

Screw high priced consultants. I decide I better start listening to my inner guidance.

GARDEN STATE INTERLUDE

Mom and Dad arrive at about 7:00 pm. They are both tired. My father had called about ten day days earlier.

"I have a court ordered mediation in San Francisco," he says.

"Yes."

"Your mother and I thought we would drive down the coast and visit you in LA when it is over."

"Great," I say.

I am thinking that it is strange to hear my father mouth the words "EL-HEY". My God, the Jersey accent is bad. "Your mother and I" means that it was her idea to begin with.

Obligatory martinis with three olives. What is it about the whole FDR generation that makes martinis the drink of choice? My mother is working on the third olive.

"Richard, tell me something."

"Yeah."

"We were driving down US 1. It is a nice drive."

"Yeah."

"And right before we got to Los Angeles, there is this place on the ocean. And there were all of these really expensive cars parked outside these little shacks."

I react in total horror.

"That is the Malibu Beach Colony. You know where the stars have their beach houses."

"Oh," my mother says. "It just looked like a bunch of shacks."

"I'll tell you what. I'll take off the day and drive you to Pasadena."

It is a long day. The grounds at the Huntington are nice.

"LA is nice, Richard," says my mother. "They have suburbs out here, just like we do in New Jersey."

"Exactly."

I drive my parents to the airport. My father turns to me immediately before he walks down the jet way on TWA flight 87 to Newark.

"San Francisco is a big nothing. All of the action is in Southern California."

MONDO CONDO

It is now fall in Los Angeles.

I can't really tell. The weather is unchanging. But my pocket calendar says "October."

I am thinking about pumpkins. I actually see a few plastic ones on my drive to the Blitstein's.

I am in the den of the Blitsteins. I am eating smoked oysters that come out of a flat can with little gold tooth picks that look like arrows from cupid's quiver, and making polite conversation with Mr. and Mrs. Blitstein.

The den is dark and filled with books, which I am pretty sure they have not read, except, of course, for the *Encyclopedia of Judaism*. This is a handy reference work, if there ever was one. Conversation is made easier by the fact that the Blitsteins have made the executive decision to let me help myself to their collection of airline miniature bottles of booze. I have successfully located two cute little bottles of Jack Daniels that look like it came from an Air Canada flight at least sometime during this decade. I am hungry and I know Chicken Vesuvius (the only dish that Mrs. Blitstein cooks for company) will be served soon. Things are good.

I look out at the deck.

"It would be nice if you had a hot tub," I say absent mindedly.

Mr. Blitstein seems impatient.

"Richard, I like to invite friends over for a meal. Not a bath."

"Oh," I say.

"In fact, it's about time for you to buy a condominium," says Mr. Blitstein.

"I don't know about that. The last time I checked, the mortgage rate was 16 percent."

"A temporary condition in the financial markets, Richard," says Mr. Blitstein. "You can't make important life decisions based upon short term interest rates. You can always refinance."

"Refinance," I repeat plaintively.

I feel my stress level going up. I like renting. It is cheap. It is so avoiding commitment.

"You need to own a little piece of the West Side of Los Angeles," says Mr. Blitstein. He is exuding financial savvy.

"You have to get on the escalator at one point or you will miss the ride to the top."

"Uh huh," I say.

I am visualizing that elevator ride to the top being a lonely one. I can do the math. After I am done paying my 16 per cent mortgage, I am going to be eating burgers in East Los Angeles without the company of the nineteen year olds who all expect to be taken to expensive bistros in Westwood.

"I am going to start looking for you on Monday, Richard."

"Thank you," I say.

I remember that arguments with Mr. Blitstein are simply pointless.

A few weeks later, I get a call to meet Mr. Blitstein at a condominium on Hilgard Avenue. Mr. Blitstein shows me a "demonstration unit." It is furnished in faux Chinese with many plastic flowers glued in vases.

"Elegant, eh?"

"Very." I say.

"They have a lot of Orientals living here?" I ask.

"I will ask," Mr. Blitstein says. "They are very good investors. This is a good building. There was a lot of bad Japanese steel being sold when this was built. I checked. They used American steel." There is absolutely no irony in Mr. Blitstein's words.

Things move very fast. Papers are signed. I visit a mortgage broker in the Valley. Most of my yearend bonus goes to the down payment and points.

"Interest is deductible," Mr. Blitstein reminds me when I am signing papers. "It is a great strength of our country," he says. I remember at one point that he told me he is a Mexican citizen.

In a matter of 22 days I own a one bedroom condominium on the fifteenth floor in Westwood in a doorman building. At least, my name is on the deed. My name is also on a $160,000 marker to the bank. One of the real estate lawyers at the firm tells me the loan is non-recourse to me personally. I am guessing that would be a good thing, if I had any other assets to protect, but I don't. Besides, the rumor about this lawyer is that he regularly eats the breakfast taco at Jack-in-the-Box.

I can't stand the wall-to-wall carpet. I take the last $5000 in my savings account and have hardwood floors installed. I also have the bedroom wall facing the bed covered in mirrors from floor to ceiling. That only costs $350. After all this is Los Angeles. The only concession to my past is the suede sofa my mother bought me in Bloomingdales.

I learn to ignore my mortgage payments and I have credit card debt for the first time in my life.

"Don't complain. You are successfully adjusting to a materialistic society," Stanford says.

I get a twenty thousand dollar raise in January. I soon retire most of my credit card debt. Judging from the price of the last one bedroom that sold in my building, I've even got equity in the apartment.

You just can't stay pessimistic in the sunshine.

AGENT ORANGE

It is 4:30 pm. I am in the firm library. I have got five different pages of the CCH Tax Reporter marked with yellow stickers. I am getting a headache.

I am paged.

"Telephone call."

"Put it through."

It is Mrs. Blitstein.

"Is everything alright?"

"Everything is fine, Richard."

"I thought something is wrong, because they paged me."

"Richard, they asked me if I wanted you paged."

"Oh. You were absolutely right to have me paged."

"Richard, I am calling." There is then a very, very pregnant pause. Then the nervous repetition.

"Richard, I am calling, because I would like to introduce you to a very nice young lady."

"Oh, thank you. I mean that is really very sweet of you," I say.

Mrs. Blitstein sounds relieved.

"Susie is the daughter of Stanford's orthodontist," she says. "He is the best orthodontist in the Valley."

Mrs. Blitstein gives me Susie's number. Susie has rejected a career in dentistry. She is a student in the graduate school in clinical psychology. She is studying at UCLA.

Without any surprise, I drive to yet another stucco three story apartment building in Santa Monica. I've got the whole UCLA housing thing down. This one has a semi-tropical sounding name, Casa de Something.

Susie turns out to be a very pretty, short brunette with a thin leather jacket and very tight jeans. She has a very inviting little butt.

Short drive down Wilshire in the direction of the high rent district and I am eating steak with Susie at Delmonico's in Westwood. Susie is eating meat, which I consider a very good sign. Susie is talking very agitatedly about Ted, who is one of her patients.

"It is all about Agent Orange," she says.

"It is?"

"It affects all of these Vietnam vets. They sprayed it everywhere. These guys are all fucked up."

"They are?

"It affects their whole psyche."

"Wow."

I figure, at this point, I should switch from questions to expletives. I notice that Susie is on her second vodka. It is having an effect.

"I hear your father is the best dentist in the Valley."

"I hate my father," she says.

"That must be hard."

I'm thinking, of course she hates her father. The guy is a god damned metal bending sadist who loves torturing teenage girls. I am very pleased with myself. I have made the shift from questions, to expletives, to expressions of empathy. I figure that Mrs. Blitstein has recited all of my academic credentials like they recite the plagues at Passover. I am mastering social interaction in Los Angeles. Less conversation is more.

Dinner is over. Suzie moves three paces in front of me, drops her handbag and gives me a butt shot that has little Richard in a very engorged state. She then grabs big Richard's arm and giggles. The pernicious effects of Agent Orange or Agent Ophelia no longer seems to be top of mind for Susie.

A short drive down Wilshire in the direction of the ocean and we are on Susie's couch at Casa de Whatever. Susie pulls a joint out of a box on the coffee table, lights it, takes a huge hit, and hands it to me.

I take a hit and in thirty seconds, I am floating. One of her patients still has good connections in Thailand. Susie takes two more hits, smiles, grabs my leather jacket and disappears. I figure she is going to pee and hang my jacket up in the closet. I am very stoned and happy. After all, one can hardly object to good housekeeping.

The second hit on the joint puts me up in the stratocumulus layer of Earth's atmosphere. I am staring at a weather balloon.

Susie reappears in front of me wearing my leather jacket, a pair of heels, and nothing else. She is yanking at my belt. Pretty soon I am on top of her with my pants around my ankles.

"Fuck me," Susie says.

Susie is screaming very loudly. In fact, a little too loudly. I start thinking about whether she has mercenaries for neighbors and whether they lust after her and whether they have automatic weapons, which they are loading at this very moment.

I kiss Susie, full on the mouth. It is the only thing I can think of to make her quiet. My field of motion is constricted, but Susie seems very happy with repetitive thrusting. She starts uttering a long series of low moans. My concerns about the mercenaries in Apartment 3A locking and loading are beginning to subside.

I get my hands around Susie's adorable little ass and we start to synchronize. This is getting to be too much for little Richard. After all, I am penetrating this girl less than twenty minutes after she confesses to me she hates her father. Big Richard starts doing multiplication tables.

"I want to bear your children," Susie says.

Big Richard decides quickly that determining the answer to 13 times 17 is not as important as this plea for procreation. Susie is very insistent.

"I want seven boys," Susie says.

Big Richard is at a loss to respond. Thankfully, Susie starts screaming really loud.

"Oh, my, God, Oh, my, God, Oh, my, God."

Big Richard manages to suppress random thoughts of screaming babies and the mercenaries in Apartment 3A, putting their Soldier of Fortune magazines in neat piles, igniting their flamethrowers and lining up for the attack. Little Richard manages to do his thing and achieve a climax.

Susie and I share a cigarette and a lot of eye contact. She is really cute. I am still wondering if this Agent Orange thing is contagious.

TALK DIRTY TO ME
ON THE CAR PHONE

I call Stanford at 3:00 pm, LA time, and tell him the story.

"My mother?" he asks.

"She says she is the daughter of your orthodontist."

"Watch out."

"What do you mean, watch out?"

"The only woman my mother ever set me up with gave me crabs."

"Well, I didn't want to offend her."

"Well, fuck my orthodontists. My teeth are all straight now."

Stanford announces he has got to go. Warsaw calling.

I am concerned. This is the most negative I have ever heard Stanford on the subject of sex. It's usually any type of sex with anybody. At any rate, I am finished talking to Stanford. I am staring at my telephone. I know that I am supposed to call Susie and I am wondering how to play this. I am pretty sure that "I like the whole seventh son of a seventh son thing" is not the way to go. I am thinking something along the lines of "I had a really great time with you last night" might be better.

The phone rings.

"Hi, it's Susie."

"I was just about to call you." Little Richard is taking over. I'm starting to get hard again.

"I'm in Daddy's Mercedes. I am calling on the car phone."

"That's great." She told me she hated her father. I am starting to get un-hard.

"I am all wet, honey. I am putting my hand down my panties. I'm playing with my pussy." Little Richard takes over. So, Susie wants to talk dirty on the car phone.

"I miss you too, honey." I am thinking "lame."

"I really want you inside me."

"Me too, honey." I am thinking "really lame."

"They are having a sale on leather pants in the Valley."

"You want me to buy you leather pants?"

"No, silly. I want to buy you leather pants."

"Honey, I'm a tax lawyer."

"I'm going to pick you up in ten minutes."

"I will be outside."

Susie shows up in the biggest, blackest Mercedes I have ever seen. And I have been in LA for months. It has a gigantic antenna on the back of the trunk. The antenna is connected to something that looks like a high voltage arrestor.

Susie smiles. She is wearing a lime miniskirt, red high heeled shoes with ankle straps, and a white filmy top. Little Richard is firmly back in control.

I get in the front seat. The motor throbs. I have to move my keys to my back pocket.

Susie drives to some warehouse in Van Nuys. Sure enough there are racks and racks of these black leather pants. There is also this vaguely Middle Eastern woman in a tight dress, which is a very odd shade of green. She is obviously presiding over this whole leather liquidation thing.

"Cute outfit," she says to Susie.

"Oh, thanks. Is there a dressing room?"

Susie grabs a couple of pairs of black leather pants. At least they are the ones that have studs only on the pockets.

"Try these on, Richard."

I am thinking that docility is the only way to get out of this. I am fantasizing about this place we passed on Ventura Boulevard where I know they serve a great Bloody Mary.

I am trying on the second pair of black leather pants. These things are impossible to put on over an erection. Susie slips discretely into the dressing room. I am trying to zipper up a pair of black leather pants that is one size too small. Susie sticks her tongue in my mouth and grabs my ass.

"Cute," she says.

Susie then drops to her knees, peels the leather pants to a level right below my ass and sticks her tongue up my asshole. She starts emitting low moaning noises. I am back in the stratocumulus layer.

Wispy cloud formations are interrupted by a knock on the door

"Can I help you with anything?" says the Middle Eastern chick from the other side of the dressing room door.

"No, No. Everything is good," I say. I am not kidding.

Suzie has lost interest in leather. I bid the green Middle Eastern chick a very polite *adieu*. In the parking lot Susie hands me the car keys.

"You drive."

No sooner than I negotiate the Mercedes out of the parking lot onto Ventura Boulevard, my pants are again below my knees and Susie is performing fellatio like she wrote the manual on it. I make it to Laurel Canyon and then turn right and to my credit I make it as far as 1145. I then have to pull into the driveway and have a wrenching organism.

Back at the condo. Susie gives me a long lingering kiss, fondles my ass, and gets back in the car to return Daddy his Mercedes Benz.

BLITSTEIN OF ARABIA

Not only is Blitstein in town for a few days, but he is going through a spiritual period.

He drops a hint that his current Polish girlfriend is insisting that he takes Yoga lessons. In any event he sounds very earnest.

"I want to drive out to the high desert."

"Where in the fuck is that?"

"Joshua Tree. It is a very spiritual place."

"I promised Susie I would spend Saturday with her."

"Bring her along."

Susie doesn't seem too sure, but I told her Blitstein is an interesting case. I intimate that he has serious problems in his relationship with his father. I neglect to say that in his father's case, it is probably a sign of normalcy. It is irresistible for a psychologist who hates her father. She takes the bait.

It is a long ride. Boys sit in the front of the bus. Susie sits in the back with the mutt. I am already regretting this. I could be back in Susie's apartment exploring my latest Penthouse fueled sex fantasies. Instead I am looking at sagebrush and an occasional scrub pine.

We reach Joshua Tree. At least Blitstein announces that we reach Joshua Tree. It all seems pretty much the same desert to me. I am not feeling spiritual, but horny. When the car stops moving I just feel hot. The temperature is 110 degrees.

Blitstein announces we are going to take a walk. Thirty minutes later we are lost in a vast wasteland. Blitstein pretends he knows where we are going. But why did it take ten minutes to get here and now it is more than forty minutes to get back?

First the dog gives up. Blitstein carries him. Susie is not happy. I see her walking in her short shorts with the snaps on the side, carrying a can of diet coke and mouthing the words *never again*. Then she goes silent. We all march on. I am reminded of T.E. Lawrence crossing the Anvil of the Sun. Even Blitstein gives up on his commentary on the purity of the desert.

I am never in my life so happy to see a VW van in need of a paint job. Even better, there is a Circle K when we reach the highway and they sell Gatorade in gallon bottles. Susie buys a six-pack of diet coke.

The drive back is mostly in silence.

I think that my mother would call this "a not particularly successful outing."

"I never want to see him again," says Susie when we finally get back to Los Angeles.

DNA

Next week is a very social week.

My next-door neighbor at the office, Kristen, invites me to a party for one of the former women litigators.

"What kind of a party is it?" I ask.

"It's a solidarity party," she says.

"Solidarity with what?" I ask. I am thinking that this has to be a woman's issue.

"Well she opened up the trunk of her car last night and she found her boyfriends body in the trunk without his head."

"No," I say.

"Yes," Kristen says.

"Supposedly he owed some money to some bad guys."

I remember meeting the guy once. He was bald and was very clearly a loser. I remember somebody told me he spent a lot of time in Los Vegas.

"I think I'll pass," I say.

Kristen pretty much expects the response.

Susie is also in the social mode. She wants to meet the people I work with. She is very insistent and good sex apparently hangs in the balance.

It is clear to me that Susie isn't taking no for an answer.

I take her to a firm party that Saturday night.

At first it seems like a pretty good idea.

We drive up in her red Alpha Romeo. The house is all of the way up in Beverly Hills. There is valet parking. The associate who drove up after me gives me a grudging look of admiration when Susie gets out with one of her shorter skirts. She has great legs.

What happens next is largely unanticipated.

Once on the sprawling patio in a sea of blue blazers, Susie makes a beeline for THE SENIOR PARTNER. I am at the bar and expecting the worse. I throw back a couple martinis in order to deal with the consequences. I summon enough liquid courage to get in hearing distance of Susie. She is engaged in an animated discussion about Herman Melville's initial failure as an author - just when I think that all Susie knows about *Moby Dick* is the size of her last Vietnam Vet boyfriend. Whatever the need to copulate with the alpha male gene is, Susie clearly has it. She is making lots of eye contact with the SENIOR PARTNER. I head back to the bar for drink number three.

I'm now chatting up the wife of the labor partner. She is wife number three and is obviously not getting enough. She is very tipsy and keeps leaning over so that I can see her very large breasts. I am pretty sure that her cavalier attitude towards their display means that they are not actually hers.

I start making "let's buzz off" gestures at Susie. Since I am now on number four, the signals are less than discrete.

When we finally get out of there, THE SENIOR PARTNER pulls me aside and tells me how much he enjoyed talking with Susie.

"She is very special," he says.

"Thank you very much," I say. I am thinking that this guy should go back home to Brentwood and scourge himself to remove impure thoughts. I also wonder for a moment how fast my career would be over if I tried to nail his seventeen-year-old daughter.

Firm politics make Susie very hot and bothered. I am too drunk to drive. She pulls over on Copa de Ora and tries to go down on me.

I'm afraid that my reaction isn't positive. I manage to get my head over the side of the car door and throw up all over the side of the Alpha.

Projectile vomiting doesn't seem to dampen Susie's newfound social enthusiasm.

Susie calls the next day. Mom wants to meet me for a drink.

I start thinking. The invitation by itself is interesting. Her daughter is 25. Drinking age for sure. Was this a way to underscore the fact that I was almost thirty? Was this a maternal warning to watch out for older guys? But this is Los Angeles. I sure don't want to think too much.

"Sure," I say. "Any day after work."

Susie's parents live in yet another large house in the far reaches of the San Fernando Valley. The Hollywood freeway is a parking lot. I finally get on the San Fernando freeway and get off somewhere in Encino. Many palm trees. Another split level house. White wine – a very nice one at that, judging from the label – is served in a sort of sunroom designed to look vaguely of Hawaiian origins. Sherry – the mother – is ensconced in a wicker chair in the corner wearing a sundress. She smiles. This is clearly meant to be a social meeting. It is not a sinister warning.

I smile warmly. Then I notice.

The mother's wine glass is wedged into a hand 2/3rd of the length of the other one with flippers for fingers.

A fucking Thalidomide victim. I begin to hyperventilate slightly. I look at Susie, but she is just being attentive.

Mom is babbling about their condo on the big island of Hawaii.

"How lovely," I say.

I am trying hard not to stare at the flipper fingers. She is now talking about how hard it is to get attentive service at the downtown Honolulu restaurants. I am trying to recall this article I read about those Thalidomide children and whether there was permanent damage to DNA.

Thankfully, a cocktail is a relatively brief affair. I don't have to answer too many questions. The fact that I am wearing a business suit seems to be enough to satisfy Dr. Susie that Daddy is working late.

Back in the Rabbit headed west towards the beach, there is no conversation about living with disabilities or support groups.

"Mom seemed to like you," Susie says. This is a girl who does not know the sacred nomenclature. She hasn't a fucking clue. I'm drifting off again and thinking about the flipper fingers of the Pinball Wizard.

Following Saturday, the Susie social program advances even further and I have tea with Susie Sister who is so excited to meet me and is happy to find that I have never been to Vietnam like the last boyfriend. It is delivered in one gasp.

Susie Sister is not bad. Same dark features. Probably a different plastic surgeon than her sister's – her nose is definitely more ski slope.

When Susie leaves discretely to relieve herself of the massive quantities of heavily flavored lemon iced tea, the Susie Sister tells me that Susie really "digs me."

I say that, "I like Susie a lot." This is obviously a good response, because Susie Sister smiles and adopts the manner of happy familiarity.

The sun is shining. I am in Venice Beach drinking tea with two skinny California sisters with styled hair and more styled noses, and at least one of which I know has a very healthy sexual appetite. When Susie and I say our good byes, only then do I notice that Susie Sister has six toes on her left foot.

After my visit to the Lanai recovery room for Thalidomide victims, I know better than to say anything. Sex with Susie was unusually perfunctory. I beg off early that night. I have a big week coming up.

That night, I have bad dreams. My only son has a tail and pointy ears. Specialists are consulted who speak about maternal bloodlines and random genetic mutations.

IMPORT EXPORT

Mrs. Blitstein invites me for dinner.

By now, I have the ritual memorized. First, smoked oysters from a can with little metal toothpicks and Ritz crackers with Swiss cheese chunks. Does she cut them up herself or do they come precut in a cellophane package from Ralphs? Dinner is iceberg lettuce with bottled salad dressing and chicken baked at 500 degrees Kelvin for a few hours and served with a sauce that is the temperature of molten lava, a dish I fondly call "Chicken Vesuvius." After dinner there are numerous cups of black coffee, fruit if you would dare eat it, and animated conversation. Coffee is a very strong diuretic and it is always a race home to the toilet after I dine with the Blitstein's.

Mr. Blitstein assumes a position on his Corinthian leather reclining chair that indicates he wants to be intimate.

"Richard, you are becoming a big success. You are working on big deals. You need to drive a better car." There is clearly a key evolutionary event going on in the Blitstein worldview. I have graduated from the Volkswagen to the Mercedes.

"I have some contacts in Germany," I say.

"Good," says Mr. Blitstein. "I will make the introduction to the converter."

Actually, I have heard about the whole racket in the pub. You buy an expensive European car for thirty percent less than the going LA price, but it is manufactured to European specification. Then you find a converter – some guy with a garage in the Valley who sticks in new headlights and grinds down mysterious things. He charges five grand, you get a pink slip and no one is the wiser.

I call an old buddy in Frankfurt who I know from my student days. He tells me that he wilk "make inquiries."

Germans are not exactly expansive when it comes to conversation.

Three weeks later the phone rings.

"I have found ze car. It is model 1978 450 SL with hard top."

"Horst, how did you do that?"

"Zis is simple. I drove to Stuttgart. I bought a newspaper. All factory workers are given the right to buy a car each year for a special price. Most buy ze car and then sell ze car."

I go to the bank the next day. I wire $13,000 to a bank account in Stuttgart whose owner was probably in the SS. It seems like a lot of money.

The bank clerk looks knowingly at me.

"Import-Export," he says.

"Right," I say. I feel important. I feel I am an international businessman.

A few weeks later a DHL envelope shows up. Inside are car keys and a bill of lading.

I feel like I am getting an assignment on *Mission Impossible*.

Next week, I feel even more like a secret agent. I receive a call from a freight forwarder in San Pedro.

"Your shipment is ready."

I have to drive to Long Beach, pick up the shipment and drive it illegally to Tustin to the mysterious "converter." I am short one driver. Who else? Susie with Daddy's Mercedes. We can caravan.

Susie seemd up for the mission. I have to take off from work.

We drive forever through the docks of San Pedro. The freight forwarder is located in a poorly marked corrugated metal shed surrounded by many other corrugated metal sheds.

I walk in. There is a knotty pine counter. A sign says "no smoking."

A helmet headed blond with a cigarette dangling out of the corner of her mouth appears. She is wearing a low cut black top and has exceedingly large breasts. I calculate north of 45 inches. She takes out her gum and sticks it under the counter.

"Bill of lading?"

I pass over the document.

"Check?"

I hand her a certified check for $750.

"The car is in the shed." She motions.

I am a little breathless when I walk through the door to the shed.

There, in the middle of the stained concrete floor, illuminated by a ray of light from a badly patched ceiling, is my gleaming white 450 SL Mercedes convertible with ze hard top.

I now own one of the sacred symbols of success.

Only then do I have a brief moment of panic. I realize I still have to face the Southern California freeway system without insurance and only the Nazi equivalent of a pink slip. I don't even have California plates. However, I am only 25 minutes from Tustin and the converter.

"Fuck it," I say to myself. I need to take more chances.

A few minutes later I am on the Pasadena freeway. Susie is in the rear mirror, smiling. She occasionally licks her fingers provocatively.

I shove an envelope full of cash at the "converter."

"Three weeks," he says.

That night I sit down with a calculator. I total acquisitions, freight forwarding, conversion, state tax, license fees. I got to about $1000 of what it would have cost me to buy the same car used off the lot at Pico and Santa Monica. I am pissed.

"Fuck it," I say to myself.

Susie just smiles.

Three weeks later I pick up the car in Tustin. I inspect it closely, but whatever the "converter" has converted isn't obvious.

I call Stanford.

"Good," he says. "You're trading up."

"Who works on the car?" Stanford asks.

"Do you recommend your guy?"

"Well, I have the vague sense that he cheats me less than he could."

I decide that is not much of a recommendation, but I go to the guy anyway.

I am impressed.

There is this guy at the entrance with a starched blue uniform and a nametag that says "OTTO." He has an authentic German accent. The waiting room has tourist magazines with headings "Tour the Rhine."

I have to go pee and I wander out the back. Everyone working the service bays is Mexican.

I am much less impressed.

I have a recruiting dinner that night. I am still feeling pretty good.

The duck is great. The law school student is pretty. Even Mike from the firm is surprisingly good company. When I walk out of Ma Maison, the night air is invigorating and my car is parked at one of the three places in the very front.

I get in and roll down the window. I take a deep drag of LA at night. Life is good. I hand the valet five bucks and get in my white Mercedes SL 450.

"You borrow your Dad's car for the weekend?" asks Mike.

LADY NARCISSUS OF PLAYA DEL REY

The next few days Susie thankfully leaves me alone. I occasionally think about what's next after tushi-lingus. By Wednesday, I am feeling entirely too dependent on the Blitstein family. My entire sex life has been taken over by Stanford, who is totally preoccupied by screwing women from the former Soviet bloc. If that isn't bad enough, when he is busy, his mother uses the opportunity to introduce me to the perverted daughters of every sadistic dentist in the San Fernando Valley.

I decide it is time to strike out on my own.

I end up in the bar at the Chart House back in the Marina. It is three minutes away from my old apartment. One of my fellow tax associates told me it had a great bar scene.

No wonder I am doing so well in the tax department. At the bar, there is me along with these two straggly dyed blonds. I sit at the corner and order a beer. My father always called it the drink of moderation.

I am lost in thought about Susie. She is going to call me again and little Richard is going to assume control and agree to meet her. I was precipitous in firing my lifestyle consultant. The next time I visit Susie in her apartment she will be wearing a latex nurse's uniform and insist on giving me an enema. In the event I resist, there will be drooling mercenaries in the closet who do nothing but smoke Thai weed impregnated with Agent Orange observing my every move through a peephole.

"Stop staring at me. It's rude."

It takes me a few seconds to determine these words are emanating from the mouth of straggle puss number 2. It takes me a few more seconds and a glance to the steroidal bartender to determine that unpleasantness must be avoided at all cost.

"I'm sorry. I am really sorry. The doctor put these drops in my eyes and I can't focus at a distance. I'm not staring. I can't even see you."

I'm thinking of Stanford's third law of attraction: any reaction is better than no reaction. Once a woman reacts you can then define the emotional content. Hate and love are both sides of the same blade, little grasshopper.

"I'm sorry."

I'm still thinking about Stanford's third law of attraction. Some Polish chick must have fed him this bullshit.

This distraction makes me sound deliberate.

"No. I'm sorry. I should have introduced myself. I'm Richard."

Straggle puss no. 1 introduces herself. It is followed by the introduction of Straggle puss no. 2. Little Richard is not taking the bait. No chemistry. This is going nowhere.

Big Richard decides he wants some comfort food. I drive to the Boy's Market in search of some comfort food. Where did the Boy hide the cookie and cracker aisle? There is nothing but green stuff.

"Can you fillet this?"

The voice is apparently speaking to me. I am pretty sure. I mean I just had one beer. It is attached to a little brunette wearing red track shorts and a tank top that says "Blitstein." She is very cute. The "B" and the "e" are both distorted.

"Are you a Blitstein?"

"No, I share a locker with her at my gym."

"Let me start over. You can filet this. In fact, I want to filet this for you."

The Blitstein brunette giggles.

The distorted "B" and "e" are inspiring me.

"No. I say. Let me start over. Please allow me to introduce myself. I'm Richard." This is a lot better than the cookie aisle. And I already practiced it once before that evening.

"I'm Genie."

"Genie, I would like to invite you for dinner where I will fillet this lovely piece of fish."

"For you," I add.

Genie is clearly thinking. I now know enough to continue to let her think.

"Well, Friday. I'm free Friday."

"This is my card. And let me write my home address."

"You live in Westwood?"

"Right."

"And you are a lawyer?"

"Right. Just like it says on the card."

Genie smiles.

Friday. Genie has traded short track shorts for a very little black dress. Very little. She bends and I see a pink thong. I'm pounding a chicken breast with the bottom of a highball glass. Genie seems impressed. I guess most guys in LA are good at cleaning and carburetor waxing surfboards. Genie appears to be a stranger to displays of testosterone in the kitchen.

Genie wants white wine. Good. No more Thai weed and pleas for insemination of multiple ovum followed by public anal sex in front of green tinted Arab women. Genie is a very sweet girl. Genie is a secretary at a company near the airport that makes weapons of mass destruction. She just broke up with her boyfriend. I feel this need to bury my head between her thighs. I do. She reacts positively. I hear muffled little moans followed by muffled "Oh, my, God's." Genie has given up smoking, so no longing glances through wisps of little clouds.

"You are very sweet to do that."

"You're very pretty. I loved to do that."

"No. I'm not."

I have an inspired moment. I take Genie to the mirror in the bathroom above the vanity. I stand behind her and slide off her dress. I whisper in her ear.

"You are beautiful."

"No."

"Look. You are beautiful."

Genie's nostrils flare. I slide the red panties to one side and enter her from behind.

Genie starts immediately with the "Oh, my, God." It is not muffled. We make eye contact in the mirror.

But mostly Genie is looking at herself. She starts playing with her breasts. She looks in the mirror. She gets more excited. She starts playing with her pussy. She looks at the mirror. She gets even more excited. I have to press her closer and closer to the mirror just to stay imbedded. She is almost pressed up against the mirror, looking at her face cross-eyed and finally she climaxes.

Genie suddenly notices that I haven't climaxed, drops to her knees and finishes me off with her mouth in a highly efficient manner. I now understand the Beach Boys when they sing "I wish they all could be California girls." I notice Genie is still looking in the mirror. Genie likes herself in profile as well. I start wondering if I have created a narcissistic monster and whether, over the long run, dealing with a leather fetish might be more manageable.

HOME MOVIES

Saturday. I drive to 96th Street, pull the car over to the side of the road and watch to planes take off to the East Coast.

Still, it is hard to stay depressed in the sunshine.

I drive back to the condo and get in the elevator. There is some blond babe wearing University of Nevada track shorts, a lime green tank top, and in-line skates.

"How's the weather?" she asks.

"Same as yesterday," I say irritably.

The eyes on the blond head attached to the lime green tank top stare at me. Nasty doesn't seem to register in Southern California outside of the bedroom.

I am still depressed, I think. I get back in the car and drive to Venice. I go to the coffee shop with no name and have bacon and eggs and toast. I like the beach. It is white and clean. I'm feeling better. I find a public phone and punch the number to my answering machine at work. One call from a midlevel partner asking about Section 306 stock. He can wait till Monday. The second call is from Lonnie – I'm transported back to baked potatos loving, sex craving stewardesses, and honey-covered penis.

"Hi, honey. It's such a nice day and I am thinking about you. Remember that time on the beach?"

In point of fact, I do not remember that time at the beach other than it is scratchy. I am not really into having sex in public places, which is what a lot of these California women think they are supposed to do. Suddenly, I am feeling cheerful. The fog is lifting, the libido is rising. I haven't seen Lonnie for a few weeks and she is probably up for anything.

I dump another quarter in the phone. An investment in my immediate future, I think. I should be writing advertising copy for Pacific Bell.

"Lonnie. It's Richard."

"Hi, Honey."

"I'm in Venice."

"I love Venice."

"Well, I would love it if you were here with me."

Lonnie giggles.

"Come down and visit me," I say.

"Oh, honey."

"Put your hand in your panties."

"Oh, Oh, honey."

"Pretend that's me, Lonnie."

Lonnie obliges by making lots of loud panting noises. I hear her roommate in the background wanting to know who ate all of the jam in the refrigerator. I make a mental note that I should write a movie treatment on "Bulimic Babes of Brentwood: they live to purge."

Lonnie takes two hours to show up. Lot's of lip gloss and eyeliner. I am on my third Corona. I neck with her for a while and she gives me a hand job in the back seat of the Pinto. She makes a point of licking all the come off her fingers while making direct eye contact with me. This girl has real potential, I think. I just need to get a video camera and borrow a few studio lights.

Two weeks later I am dispatched to New York for a due diligence meeting. I am probably being punished by the MID LEVEL CORPORATE PARTNER who I did not call back on Saturday. It turns out the company has some really funky stuff going on with one of its Dutch subsidiaries. I distinguish myself. The underwriter makes them undo all of the tax sharing arrangements as a condition to taking them public. The head of my department invites me to his corner office to compliment me. That's all nice. But what I really like is that I get out of the meeting early enough to get to Canal Street and buy a high resolution video camera.

I am now instrumented and motivated, but lack opportunity. A couple of not so subtle hints about Lonnie auditioning produces nothing but giggles and "I want to kiss it for you."

I resolve to wait patiently. It turns out I don't have to wait too long.

On the 29th day of the month, Lonnie calls. After a minute of the "miss you honey" stuff she gets to the point.

"My roommate didn't come up with the rent money." Lonnie sucks in a breath.

"How much?" I ask.

"300."

"Oh."

"Can you help?"

"Yeah sure."

"But I need it now."

"Now?"

"The landlord says if he doesn't have the rent in cash by 4:00 pm today, he is going to give me some kind of official notice."

I know enough about the California law of eviction from Mr. Affray and my secretary to know this is bullshit.

"But, Lonnie, it's almost noon." I'm thinking the landlord is going to make Lonnie and her roommate an offer at 4:00 pm regarding how they can earn the rent that has nothing to do with official notices.

"Please. I'm going to do anything you want."

"OK, OK."

I am moving very quickly at this point. I pull out 15 twenties from the Bank of America branch in the basement of the building. I put them in an official looking envelope. I have Lisa type Lonnie's address and stamp the envelope: LEGAL DOCUMENTS – PERSONAL AND CONFIDENTIAL. I then make a beeline to the messenger department. I tell Ramon that we need to talk privately. Ramon pumps iron and puts out vibes like he would fuck the coin return slot of a coca cola machine. For a twenty he agrees to drive immediately to Brentwood to drop off an envelope to Ms. Evans on a very important matter. I wonder why these Jewish girls in LA always have these I-spy names, and I think of Norma Jean.

Ramon reports two hours later that the mission is accomplished. There is a big smile on his face.

"Anytime, Mister Richard, anytime," Ramon says.

Ramon's protestations of fealty make me suspicious. I call Lonnie.

"Did you get your package?" I say the word "package" very distinctly.

"Thank you, Honey. The messenger you sent was really nice. Sally and I had a coke with him."

"What were you doing?"

"We were just sunbathing on the patio."

"I'll see you tonight."

"Ok, honey."

Lonnie and Sally, as I have previously determined from close inspection, sunbath topless. I'm sure Ramon is looking forward to the end of next month.

As for my career as a pornographer, it turns out to be extremely short lived. Lonnie really considers it as a screen test and babbles about her high school play before giving me a reluctant blow job. I slap her bottom a few times and she gets a little more animated. We never end up watching the tape together. After I come, I escort Lonnie to the door. I notice there is yet another spot on my suede couch.   There could be more here.

PROFESSOR KINK

Now that I have Lonnie captured on videotape, I now understand why the Navaho Indians refuse to have their pictures taken from the fear of stolen souls. Whenever I am tempted by the prospect of tryst with Lonnie, five minutes of Channel 3 either quickly convinces me otherwise or provides me the opportunity for relief. It is infinitely preferable to the whole three hour, Caesar-salad-baked-potato followed by the I-hate-my-bank-job ritual. Sex is characterized by entirely too much pelvic thrusting. Afterplay always consists of pillow talk oriented around the twin concepts of flying with the airlines and having million dollar babies.

I do realize one evening that I talked more to Blitstein while he was in Boston and less now that he's in the same metropolitan statistical area.

I reach him at his office.

"I have one of my colleagues with me, Richard. I would like to introduce her to you."

"Oh," I say.

"Kathy Cheesky, meet Richard Parker."

We have drinks in Westwood. Assistant Professor Cheesky was born in Romania. She speaks Romanian and French. Her area of research is the effect of the industrial revolution on the role of Romanian women in postmodern society. She has a nice laugh and extremely large breasts.

Kathy lives in some faculty housing development that looks like every other housing development in LA, except with more Volvos.

She pours me a glass of white wine.

"I like you," she says.

"I like you."

She has made some kind of Romanian chicken dish for dinner. Conversation is pleasant. She clears away the dishes. I am thinking that these Eastern European types may present some advantages.

Why don't you go into my bed room, open up the second shelf of the chest of drawers and find something you like and I will put it on for you," she says.

The second drawer of Dr. Kink's dresser is like the Oxford Library of underwear. Someone has done her own personal inventory of every item sold at Frederick's of Hollywood since 1947. There are pairs of crotchless panties in every color of the rainbow, matching open nipple bras, garter belts, boas, and seamed stockings. You can wardrobe the photo shoots for a fetish magazine for the next twelve months from just one drawer. And there were three drawers. Somebody left Romania with hard currency. I pick out a matching bra, panty and stockings outfit and leave it in the middle of the bed. It is all black and red. I hope Dr. Kink isn't hung up on tied dyed panties.

When I return to the living room, there is a bottle of brandy on the coffee table. French, not Romanian. Dr. Kink gives me a little peck on the cheek.

"Give me fifteen minutes," she says.

I pour a drink and clear my mind. Blood is flowing to the nether regions.

Dr. Kink is inspired.

She is propped up on a satin pillow. Her legs are spread. In the candlelight I see that she has not only made up her lips with very red lipstick, but also her labia. Her nipples are erect.

Foreplay doesn't seem indicated. I penetrate her and begin moving forcefully in and out. She starts moaning and grinding back.

"I've been naughty," says Dr. Kink.

"Very naughty."

"I need a spanking."

I pull out, flip her over and look at the broad expanse of her ass. It is pretty, framed by the black garters. I slap her. She moans. I slap her again. She is arching her back so her ass gets closer to my hand. The moan turns into a higher pitch squeal. Her ass starts getting very red.

"Please," she says.

"Tell me where you want it," I say.

I decide I am really getting into this whole violation thing, but nowhere near as much as Dr. Kink.

"In my ass. In my ass. I need your cock up my ass."

Well, I am not going to argue about anal sex with the girl who looted Fredericks. I give her an ass pounding that a Greek soldier would be proud of. I come a little too dramatically, but the whole thing seems a little staged so I want to play my part.

Dr. Kink slides off to the bathroom. I go out to the balcony to smoke. The Dr. Kink household is tolerant of anal penetration, but not tobacco products.

Dr. Kink announces that she wants me to have dinner with her parents next weekend.

Well, I think, nothing this good comes without conditions.

I RETURN TO THE
LAIR OF DR. WRONG

I have a long history with Nathalie Wright.

I met her at a law school party on the first day of class in the beginning of my third year. She had long legs and a very short skirt – a deadly combination for me in itself. It got worse after I discovered a bottle of Jack Daniels and Jack started telling me that chatting up the long legged, short skirted brunette was a good idea. Little Richard was fully in control of the program.

"So, who are you?"

"I'm Nathalie Wright."

"So, what do you do?"

"I'm at the Med school."

"You're going to be one cute doctor."

Nathalie leaned over and kissed me. Two tongues met, and, as they say, the rest is history.

Of course, Blitstein immediately began calling her "Dr. Wrong." He also started screwing Nathalie's best friend - a dyed blond who graduated from Smith and trained at Boston Memorial to deliver "million dollar babies." I have to admit, Nathalie did have a bad habit of giving me prescription psychotropic drugs to take when she wanted to modify my behavior. Nathalie and I parted ways shortly after I got to Los Angeles. As a matter of fact, she picked me up at the Los Angeles airport and our relationship was over by the time we hit the Pasadena freeway. However, it is difficult to lose old friends in Los Angeles. There is something about relations with women that begin on long winter nights in front of real flames in the fireplace after much conversation. These relationships just seem harder to give up then the ones that begin with a tacky one liner in the blinding sunshine.

Nathalie is sitting on my favorite suede couch in the Mondo Condo. Which actually doesn't look too bad given the wear and tear. If the sales lady in Bloomingdales had any clue what was going to happen on this thing when I bought it, she would have called the CDC in Atlanta. Nathalie is an intern now at County General and working crazy hours. Nathalie is looking for my insight on how to bust up the relationship of this MARRIED SURGEON that she wants for herself. Nathalie is extremely direct.

"Well, I spent the night last Friday. I went into the medicine cabinet and I rearranged all of her make up."

"Just to let her know you were there?"

"Of course. You got any better ideas?"

"Leave your panties under the bed. Red ones."

"I like that," Nathalie squeals. "I'm going to fuck you."

Nathalie takes my hand and escorts me to the bedroom. She straddles me and begins grinding. I am very passive. I look at the event in the mirrored sliding closet doors. It feels like this is happening to somebody else. I wonder vaguely if Lady Narcissus of Playa del Rey has permanently screwed up my synapses. I try to remember if psychiatric treatment is covered on my health plan.

Nathalie issues little yelps. I follow with a groan. Actually, it is almost a sigh of relief.

"Can you think of anything else?" she asks.

"A silk bathrobe is always nice."

"You fucking anybody else?"

I look at Nathalie disapprovingly.

There is something inherently erotic in unanswered questions. Nathalie shows up more often. Lots of quiet little yelps. She seems to enjoy inspecting my member before she goes down on me. A frustrated dermatologist, but I wonder how many women actually get to play doctor with their boyfriends' penises.

Things with THE MARRIED SURGEON are not going so well. He is tired and distracted. It seems that while wielding his scalpel a couple people have died and he is beginning to doubt his ability to communicate directly with God. I am sympathetic. Nathalie is not a lot fun if you are suffering from even the slightest little bit of self-doubt. Empathy is not one of her gifts. All this scheming has brought Nathalie and me closer together. I have a suspicion that my performance is better than THE MARRIED SURGEON who has to spend ten hours a day on his feet dealing with naked palpitating organs with bad stuff in them. It's Saturday morning and Nathalie has spent an even longer than normal period of time inspecting my member.

"We should move in together."

"What?"

"No. Where?"

I am already lost. Nathalie has found this housing project on Avenue 56, right off the Pasadena Freeway. Not the greatest neighborhood on the East Side.

"But Police Chief Gates lives there," Nathalie says. "It will be very safe."

Nathalie is very pragmatic. Urban renewal prices are ok, as long as they come with a guaranteed SS regiment of personal security troops to prevent incursions by Blacks and Hispanics. Moreover, Nathalie is not just pragmatic. She directs all the bioelectrical energy generated by her brain to the scheming center of her very large frontal lobe to work through the parameters of her new project. I am to be assaulted on all fronts, and, as Nathalie knew every strategic vulnerability of her target, the campaign promises to be short and decisive. Nathalie knows what she wants, so, I think, "what do I want?"

Well, I have read the Harold Robins novel during my distant adolescences where the protagonist is given to snorting caps of amyl nitrate to prolong his orgasms. I tell Nathalie about it. She shows up next weekend with four glass ampoules.

"I hate you," she says.

"Come on Nat, this is going to be great."

"You don't understand. This shit has exactly one therapeutic indication. I did the research. I went to the pharmacy a couple minutes before they closed and I told the pharmacist that I had this patient who is presenting weirdly and I needed to make an additional diagnosis."

"Perfect."

"And then he says, 'You got a boyfriend, Nat? You want poppers?'"

"Oh," I say.

Poppers are ok. After making the beast with one back, cracking open the fourth and final ampoules, and collapsing to the side of my little physician, she looks at me sweetly.

"So you want to make it with another girl and me?"

"How did you know?"

"All you guys have the same fantasy."

A week later I am making a bottom round roast at the condo. Nathalie shows up with Nurse Tina. Nurse Tina is wearing pink track shorts and frizzy blond ringlets. I can barely get a little white wine in glass for Nurse Tina, when Nathalie's beeper goes off.

"Shit," Nathalie says. "I need a phone."

The phone call takes place in those hushed medical tones. The patient is filling up with some kind of fluid.

"I have to go to County. I got a patient in bad shape."

Nathalie gives me a long, very wet kiss and squeezes my cock.

"Tina likes you. I wanted this to be a three way, but you get started. I'll be back in a couple of hours."

Nurse Tina is nowhere to be found in my dining room or the living room. I locate her in my bed, stark naked, her blond ringlets carefully arranged on the pillow.

"Nathalie says that we are all going to do it together, but I thought I should get to know you first." She says it very sweetly. This, I found very compelling logic.

Nurse Tina is not only technically gifted but has obviously taken extra courses in the important nursing skill of mouth to penis resuscitation. I want to use her every orifice, but I am overcome by exhaustion before I can make it to her bottom. Nathalie shows up the next morning. She lost her patient and looks tired. She puts on a bathrobe and is particularly affectionate with Nurse Tina over breakfast, licking jam off of her nipples. I am content to watch. Nurse Tina seems to have sapped most of my life force from her ministrations the night before. Nathalie is too tired to get into the whole Lesbian thing.

Nathalie announces that Nurse Tina needs a ride back to County General and I am going to take her. I see Nathalie slip her hand down the back of Nurse Tina's track shorts when she kisses her goodbye.

It is a pretty quick drive. If I didn't have a stick shift I'm sure Nurse Tina would have climaxed a few more times. When I get back, Nathalie is just drifting off to sleep.

"Did you get the contract?" she asks.

I nod.

"Then, go buy us a house, sweetie."

First, I call Sally's mom, who listed the Mondo Condo and managed to get it into contract three days later. I now had enough to match Nathalie's contribution to the down payment.

As Nathalie has correctly calculated, the prospect of owning an edifice jointly with her, a center where naughty nurses would minister to both of its co-owners, is a concept that is impossible to resist. My fantasy life has reached overdrive by the time I take the exit off the Pasadena Freeway to the sales office. I stare at the model floor plans and I notice the garage is quite large. I make a mental note that it can be easily converted into a classroom where Nathalie would instruct scores of nurses - all dressed in short little uniforms with white stocking, garter belts, and little hats - on the correct method of worshiping the male organ. I would, of course, be personally responsible for administering final exams. I check all the boxes for upgrades: better linoleum, better tile in the kitchen, a little brick veneer out front, and even the deluxe garage door opener. I want Nathalie to feel happy in her new home.

The next Monday, I take out the contract and my calculator and figure out how long it would take to pay for all of this. The results, even adjusted by tax savings, show human bondage of many years.

When I arrive at home, Nurse Tina is descending the staircase. Nathalie's attachment to Nurse Tina is no longer to stimulate little Richard, but has apparently taken on it a dynamic of its own.

I don't care. I have a headache. I need to talk with Nathalie about what were going to do extract ourselves from this era of condo induced poverty.

"Honey, can you make me a cup of tea?" I say.

"I'm a doctor," snapped Nathalie. "Make it yourself."

Of course, from twenty-twenty hindsight, this is the beginning of the end. Nathalie and I lasted another couple of months. We decorate together, sleep together and I even come to the cafeteria at County General when she is on call and eat powdered eggs. One evening I come home and Nathalie and Nurse Tina were giving each other bikini waxes. Nathalie announces she has vacation days and she and Nurse Tina are going on a cruise.

I put an ad in the *LA Times* the next day: "Divorce forces sale of luxury condo."

It was almost true.

VOTA RAÚL

I am now deeply depressed. At least when I was living with Dr. Wrong, I could at least tell myself that I was in a relationship that was merely going through a difficult period. Now I have all the disadvantages of divorce without ever being married. I even have a bad property settlement. I am left with the CCH Tax Reporter, and not even the head of the tax department can find the meaning of life in the internal revenue code.

Blitstein picks me up at 8:00 am. I am in the middle of the living room with my four suitcases and a very melancholy expression. Blitstein rings the doorbell - another upgrade I haven't paid for. I will be paying for the linoleum and the Belgian granite countertop until I am 40. At that moment my ex-girlfriend descends the staircase wearing a black negligee and high heeled red shoes. Dr. Wrong is extremely charming, inquiring as to what Blitstein has been up to and questioning him intently on his current research interests. I drag the bags off to Blitstein's car. I notice Nathalie's nipples are erect.

I give Dr. Wrong a kiss good bye.

"Be good," she says.

That is something I have no intention of.

Four hours later, I have moved into a one bedroom apartment in Studio City. I am writing out the check for the security deposit to yet another helmet headed fifty something. I am back in the San Fernando Valley.

"That little bitch was coming onto me," Blitstein says. "I never realized she had such nice tits."

I am too depressed to respond.

"This is a great location," Blitstein continues in a vain attempt to cheer me up. "All these aspiring actresses live here. Man, the movie studios are all here. You can discover an actress even before the studios do." Blitstein is overcome by his own rhetoric.

I spend my first night away from Dr. Wrong – well, not counting the nights on call – in four months. I am drifting into another dreamless sleep in my new mattress, which was delivered only a few hours before. All I did was call an 800 number. Suddenly, I hear a scream.

I go out to the balcony, which overlooks the swimming pool as it does in every apartment building in Los Angeles. Blackness. There is one light on in the last row of first floor apartments facing me. The door opens. Six Japanese guys, all in business suits with white shirts and narrow black neckties, are carrying cameras with very large flash devices, marching down the hall in single file. I go back to sleep.

Next morning I go to the Circle K to get a cup of coffee. The guy in line ahead of me is about six-foot-three and is wearing a full beard and a sundress with yellow flowers.

I am having transition issues with my new neighborhood.

Blitstein picks me up at noon. He is driving his father's car – a gigantic Oldsmobile diesel with a supplemental 100 gallon tank in the back. Blitstein explains that we could drive to Cabo San Lucas and back without having to purchase gas from a Mexican. I detect the finely developed mind of Mr. Blitstein in these automotive modifications. There is only one species of Mexican – they obviously cannot be trusted with gasoline. I think about asking Stanford whether he has brought a portable fallout shelter.

"How are you, Richard?"

"Stanford, I have descended to the fourth level of hell. I have lost my girlfriend – the same girlfriend who made me move to Los Angeles and encouraged me to fuck her lesbian lovers. Now I have moved to the San Fernando Valley and I am living among the victims of sadistic Japanese pornographers and radical cross dressers."

"Come on, Richard," says Stanford, poo-pooing the whole thing. "You know Dr. Wrong is evil. She is bad for you. Cheer up. Did you know that Captain Kirk lives right down the block from you?"

Blitstein is headed down the 405. I realize that he is traveling South – the direction of the third world. He peels off on Century Boulevard.

"You need diesel?" I ask. I start doing the mental math about how many miles we could get before we would exhaust a 120 gallon tank. I was already near Mexico City.

"No, we are going to pick up Maria."

Maria is San Juan via Harvard College. She has a nice smile. She doesn't speak too much English. Blitstein assures me that she will be invaluable once we cross into Mexico and have to interact with natives. I curl up in the back of the Oldsmobile and go to sleep.

When I wake up we are in Encinitas. Maria has become much more animated and is interacting with the locals. We end up in a steak restaurant near a pretty clean looking hotel. I am on *cervesa* number four.

"You are coming out of it," Blitstein says. "You look much better."

"No. I am still in a major depression. I'm just feeling less pain because of the alcohol."

Maria makes it clear she has enough of the red meat, beer and depression-inspired male bonding. She splits for the hotel.

The beer is not helping. I go to a bodega and buy a bottle of El Presidente. This is the brandy of the conquistadors, I think. It will solve the problem.

Blitstein is on a tear. He has been talking real fast and is real excited. Dr. Wrong is not only evil - she is satanic. She is the spawn of the devil and a field hockey coach at a second rate prep school in a déclassé suburb of Detroit. Not only did she come on to him, she will attempt to sleep with anyone who ever befriends me regardless of their sex as long as I live. Moreover, she gave me noxious chemicals that only doctors knew about to prevent me from having an erection. After being rendered impotent, she then brought her Lesbian girlfriends over and had sex with her in front of me with strap-on dildos in order to humiliate me. Blah, blah, blah.

I now switch from cerveza to the real thing. The liquid level in the El Presidente bottle is now down to the "P." I am definitely feeling better.

Blitstein has a belt of El Presidente. He stops his tirade about Dr. Wrong for a few minutes.

I spot a poster for the local PRI candidate for Mayor. It says "Vota Raúl."

"Vota Raúl," I say. I raise my paper bag with its bottle in a toast.

I am getting much less concerned with the whole Dr. Wrong chapter of my life.

A pedestrian approaches on the street.

"Vota Raúl," I say somewhat more forcefully.

"Vota Raúl," agrees Senor Pedestrian.

I seem to remember that there is only one political party in Mexico. How wrong can I go? I make my way to the main square where there are more people who need to be reminded how to vote.

I have no clear recollection of how I got to the hotel or in bed.

The next day I have one of the worst hangovers I can remember for a very long time. There is no Dr. Wrong to give me drugs. I am still miserable. I lay on the beach and drink bottles of mineral water. I am now a light shade of crimson, but thankfully no longer hung-over.

Maria has some kind of family problem and has to fly back to San Juan. As best I could tell, her brother has been arrested in San Juan for joy riding. I am impressed that she has managed to negotiate the Mexican telephone system. We are all back in the Oldsmobile headed North. We cross the border. Blitstein is again in one of his irrepressible good moods, turns the radio on, and starts playing Mariachi music.

Blitstein forgets to bring his Canadian passport. I'm sure it has expired anyway. Maria says that she thinks she has a Puerto Rican driver's license in the trunk.

A customs official with a gigantic flashlight waives us over. The thing must take 19 "D" cells. He has very white teeth and his shirt has a lot of starch in it. The Mariachi music is blaring. The customs official shines his flashlight.

"Everybody here a U.S. citizen?"

"Si, Senor," says Blitstein.

The customs official gives Blitstein a disgusted look and waives him on past the barbed wire and searchlights.

I'm starting to think I don't take enough chances.

TEENAGE ENEMA
NURSES IN BONDAGE

Blitstein is back in town for a few days.

We have breakfast at Ships coffee on Westwood Boulevard.

"I picked up this nurse on the plane coming in last night," he says.

"So?"

"She's cute. She is the right size for you. And I haven't got time."

"So?"

"You call her."

"What am I suppose to say?"

"Tell her that you were having breakfast with me and that I suggested you give her a call."

"Call for what?"

"To have coffee. Richard, sometimes I worry about you. You lack imagination. This is Los Angles. People connect with people. Call and ask her to have coffee."

Later that day, I call. Jennifer Liebowitz is moving back to Los Angeles after eighteen months in Boston. She is living with her parents in Brentwood until she can find a place.

We have coffee in Westwood the next day.

Jennifer is a lot of fun to talk to. She hates Boston. It is filled with unwashed interns who can't stop hitting on her when they find out she is from California. She is a bizarre combination of a nurse and a Jewish American Princess. During a class on how to make hospital corners she asks, "Doesn't the maid do that?" Turns out she spent three weeks nursing Richard Pryor back to life after he tried to burn himself to the ground with a crack pipe. She says she is very good with positive eye contact.

She is right. Her eyes are dark brown pools that are starting to arouse little Richard into his dangerous erectile state.

When I drop her off, she invites me in to meet Daddy.

Daddy is a dermatologist. Seems he is the man to talk to when you get a pimple in the middle of a shoot. I make a mental note in case I have an important closing and a zit forms on my nose.

Daddy also plays the stock market buying medical device manufactures.

I offer to get him a couple of quarterly reports.

When I drop them off a few days later, he seems very appreciative. I guess he doesn't understand that a firm client is really paying for this stuff.

I use the occasion to ask his daughter out to dinner.

We have a perfectly civil meal. I drink a little too much and talk about how female undergarments from the 1950s are the ultimate turn on. I bemoan the fact that you can't find real fetish magazines anymore.

Jennifer's nostrils start to flare slightly.

We end up in the basement of her parent's house. They have a fireplace you can turn on with something that looks like a garage door opener. It is very romantic, even though I keep thinking about an article in *Sunset* magazine about the advantages of having a rumpus room and wondering if this were one. The necking turns into petting, and I manage to get my hand far enough into Jennifer's panty hose in order to bring her to what appeared to be quite a wrenching orgasm.

Reciprocation is obviously a well engrained instinct in the Liebowitz family, because Jennifer is literally attacking my zipper. My pants are very soon around my ankles and I am getting a very skillful and very pleasant blow job. I wish I could see better. Suddenly I hear the rumble of an automatic garage door and the Daddy type inquires about what is going on.

Jennifer removes my penis from her mouth long enough to say, "Richard and I are just talking."

I manage to come shortly thereafter. I would have resisted, but the proximity of Daddy Doctor is preying on my super ego and dampening my ardor.

I suggest that maybe Jennifer would like to visit me at my apartment during our next tryst.

She seems amenable.

Saturday night.

I do pasta with shrimp.

After dinner we snuggle on the couch. Just necking. I'm thinking that I should pretend that I haven't already practically fucked her. I put Berlin on the stereo. They are definitely right, "Nobody Walks in LA."

The first side of the album is over.

Jennifer gets up.

"Let me do it," she says. "I just feel like serving you."

She smiles and lifts up her skirt. She is wearing a garter belt and red mesh panties cut out in the shape of a heart.

I am in love.

Jennifer is again attacking my zipper and very soon I journey forth to the planet Califellatio.

Jennifer has to leave at midnight. Living with parents isn't such a bad thing, I am thinking. I start to wonder about how fresh the shrimp actually were. Tossing and turning next to a strange clingy body is not a pleasant end to an otherwise perfect evening.

Sunday morning.

There is ringing. The alarm clock reads 8:05 am. It is light outside.

I have a migraine headache. It's like I have on two pairs of glasses and a pair of contact lenses. I can't take them off. Somebody is pounding on the top of my head.

The ringing is not coming from the alarm clock. It is coming from the telephone.

It's the doorman.

"It's your lady friend," says the doorman.

"Thank you."

I unlock the door and crawl back to bed.

Jennifer appears suddenly in the doorway to the bedroom.

From what I can make out through the three pairs of lenses that somebody has glued on my eyeballs, she is wearing her nurse's uniform with a little white hat. That hat has a red cross on it. It looks a little fuzzy around the edges.

"I've got a migraine," I say.

"I just spent an hour putting on this outfit and you are going to fuck me," Jennifer says.

Jennifer starts licking my toes. In a few minutes she has worked her tongue up to the crack of my ass.

Somebody is still pounding on the top of my head, but I have an erection.

Jennifer lifts up her uniform. She is wearing white stockings and a frilly little garter belt, but no panties. She straddles me and starts rocking back and forth. She is moaning. Then she is moaning louder.

I am starting to think that this is her fantasy and not mine, but the pounding is getting a little softer. The blood rushes from my head to my penis. Somehow my prostate starts to convulse and so do I. I climax. It appears that Jennifer has already done so – and evidently more than once.

I am feeling better.

Jennifer gets up and makes coffee.

This time she is more direct. She takes me in her mouth and I see her nurse's cap start bobbing up and down around my mid section. I look in the mirror wall facing the bed and I have a nice view of her ass framed by the stocking and the hem of her skirt.

I have an inspiration.

"Nurse, your patient requires more anal attention," I say.

Jennifer takes a little gasp, but soon her little tongue is darting in and out of my rectum. Somehow she manages to reach my penis and give me a hand job at the same time.

At this point, I am leaning on the side of the bed. I turn around and take another glimpse at the mirror. I am congratulating myself on my decorating skills and I climax again.

I find Jennifer in the bathroom vigorously brushing her teeth.

"You OK?" I ask.

"You didn't fleet or anything," she says. "Did you ever hear of E-coli?"

I laugh. I realize I should be more sympathetic. They are actually a lot of germs in hospitals.

Visiting nurses are OK, I think.

THE DISCO DENTIST

Three days later I have a toothache.

I have had toothaches before, but this is the mother of all toothaches. Much worse than a hangover. I realize it has been a year since I saw the dentist in Pasadena. I remember that Dr. Good has recommended him and I also remember I don't like him.

There is something about dental pain that makes you do crazy things.

I call Jennifer.

"I will call Daddy," she says.

Five minutes later I have the name of some dentist on Rodeo Drive in Beverly Hills who will see me the minute I walk into the office.

I am starting to think I am in love.

The dentist is a young guy. He is wearing one of those Hawaiian shirts with a gold chain. He looks like somebody who would hang out in a Disco.

"Nasty," he says.

"Is that a technical term?"

The Disco Dentist just laughs.

He shoots me up with something. In about a minute, I am pain free. In about three minutes, I am feeling good.

The familiar buzzing of a dental drill and about twenty minutes later the Disco Dentists pronounces that he is done.

He takes me to his office. I am still a little woozy, but trying to be nice to the man who took my pain away.

"May I speak frankly?" asks the Disco Dentist.

"Sure," I say. I am hoping the guy gives me pills or something. I just don't think I can take that level of pain again.

"I can really do some nice stuff with your smile," he says.

I look blankly.

"If I were to yank that second left incisor and overfill the remaining teeth, you would look great," he says.

"Really?"

"Like a move star."

"And how much?"

"Less than $6,000. It would be a real investment in your future."

I am thinking that the Disco Dentist is starting to sound like the Mercedes salesman. Why are these sales guys in Los Angeles always telling me that consumption is investment? Maybe here it is.

"I'll have to think about it."

"Do that," says the Disco Dentist and flashes his own $6,000 smile.

My own bill for my misfortune comes to $600. I am not happy, but the memory of the pain is still vivid. I try to think of it like a car accident.

TWISTED SISTER

Things are not going well with Jennifer.

She seems increasingly unhappy at being mounted like a mountain goat. There are snappy little comments like she expects me to look at her during the act of intercourse. Finally, she has the temerity to complain that I am not spending the entire night after I left at 5:00 am, spending 11:00 pm to midnight slapping her bottom until it was all the same perfect color of pink.

I have a sense that all of these annoyances can be resolved by professions of commitment. That thought, of course, rouses in me a primordial urge to flee.

At work, I have a voicemail from Dee, who is Jennifer's older sister.

It takes me a few days, but I call back.

"I was waiting for your call," says Dee. She sounds a little breathless.

"I'm sorry. Too much work. You know." I remember that she is a paralegal. I figure that is one excuse she might actually believe – lawyers complaining about overwork.

"When we talked at my parents, I thought we said we were going to get together since we were both downtown?"

"Yeah. We do have to do that."

"What about tonight? Just stop on the way home. I'll make you something for dinner."

The implications of this invitation dawned on me only when I rang the doorbell.

Yet another tacky apartment complex where Beverly Hills meets West Hollywood. This one has very lush vegetation and vaguely winding stairways with faux wrought iron to the second floor.

I had not picked up on the fact that Dee had such large breasts – very large, perky ones that are three quarters exposed in a very skimpy bathing suit top. The outfit is completed by cutoff shorts that leave the crack of her ass highly defined with heels.

"You caught me gardening," Dee says.

"I'm sorry," I say. I decide to take the remark at face value. In point of fact, this is an outfit suitable for raising Venus flytraps and not much else.

"Just a minute. Let me put on the pasta. Here's a vodka."

I sit in a very oversize brown armchair. I observe the art. It is modernistic and very tortured. I am slowly recovering from work and the drive here. I'm starting to feel better.

Every few minutes I get a glimpse of Dee's denim covered derrière. I am starting to feel much better. I realize this deliberate exhibitionism comes with implications I probably don't want to deal with, but I am too mentally exhausted to think about it.

Dinner is good. Pasta has a very nice cream sauce. I taste a hint of vodka, or that could still be the vodka I have been sucking on for the last thirty five minutes.

After dinner, I retire to the cushy brown armchair I have made home. Dee sits at my feet with her chin on my thigh.

"You know, I never met anybody who could stand up to my parents."

"I'm just a little older."

"No, they like you. My father seems to respect you."

"That maybe, or he may be pretending," I say.

Dee suddenly gets up.

"I've got 'ludes," she says. She sounds excited.

I am thinking that the last time I took a Quaalude, it was on a road trip to Syracuse, New York. I spent four hours feeling like I was walking under water. I think at one point I had to go to the emergency room for frostbite, but I really didn't care.

She literally pops one in my mouth and follows it with a kiss.

I have fleeting thoughts. *This is my girlfriend's sister that I am about to fuck - my girlfriend is not going to happy about this when she finds out - in all probability she will find out - we will have a giant emotional mess.*

Dee is now rubbing my crotch. She pulls my pants down to my knees and is placing little kisses over the head of my penis. I do not remember much else.

Next morning I wake up to the sound of Dee on the telephone explaining to her supervisor that she will be late for work. I check in with my secretary and there are no crises that I cannot deal in two hours.

Dee hands me a very strong cup of coffee for which I am very thankful.

She is wearing red heels and red panties. Nothing else.

"What happened?"

"You were a real tiger. Don't you remember? I fell off the bed."

As a matter of fact, I don't remember very much of anything after the oral sex session on the cushy brown armchair, but Dee seems very satisfied. I again have a brief flash of memory that this sexually obedient young woman, happened, in fact, to be the sister of my girlfriend.

"About last night," I say.

Dee starts licking my balls and works her warm little mouth to the head of my penis. She clearly doesn't want to talk. I decide to shut up and come.

DUELLING SUPERVIXENS
OF THE VALLEY

The next Friday night.

I decide that I am going to work on the commitment issue with Jennifer by indirection.

She shows up with a little pink overnight bag and announces she needs some time to get dressed up.

That, of course, is the perfect opportunity for Richard to pull out the bong behind the plunger under the kitchen sink, and to reach a level of calculated indifference when she reappears. Richard realizes that he is not going to spoil this evening by dealing with the sister issue. In fact, it may be better to ignore the whole sister issue forever.

Jennifer appears dressed as the Fredrick's of Hollywood version of a French maid, complete with a white, frilly apron and black see through panties.

"Cute," I say.

Jennifer is adjusting her garters. "I want to serve you."

Jennifer starts licking my toes and slowly works her tongue up my leg.

Jennifer is getting into this whole servitude thing and is moaning. I start moaning, because I am getting into Jennifer getting into the whole servitude thing. I grab her hair and drag her into the bedroom. At this point, Jennifer is licking the bottom of my scrotum and I am anticipating a nice wet little lunge, inching its way to my butthole.

I hear a knock at the door.

"Shit."

"Who can that be?" Jennifer says.

I am struggling for rational thought.

"It's just somebody at the right door on the wrong floor."

Jennifer appears mollified.

I grab a towel and open the front door a crack.

It's Dee.

She is wearing a French maid's costume and holding a feather duster. This one is a little more abbreviated. In fact, both of her tits are hanging out of the top. She has rouge on her nipples.

"I'm here to make clean." Dee is smiling.

"Bad, Bad timing. How did you get in here?"

"I gave the doorman twenty bucks."

"You've got to go now." I am getting agitated.

The next few minutes elapse in slow motion.

I am vaguely aware that Jennifer is standing behind me. She reaches under my arm, grabs Dee by the hair and drags her into the apartment. Jennifer lets out a shriek, head butts Dee in the stomach and drops her to the floor.

"You bitch, you fucking bitch. This is my boyfriend."

Jennifer is now straddling Dee and pummeling her head.

I am paralyzed.

Two valley girls dressed in lingerie are in one of the great cat fights of all time – and it's all over me.

Dee is recovered from Jennifer's initial onslaught and starts fighting back. She rolls on top of Jennifer and starts beating on her tits. I get an awesome beaver shot.

Jennifer manages to get a round house off to the side of Dee's face.

I see blood and I snap out of advanced voyeurism into action. I pull the two girls off of each other.

"Out of here. Both of you, out of here."

Both girls pick up their things, put on their raincoats and leave. There is silence.

I pour myself four fingers of Jack Daniels and think. I decide that simply ignoring developments is not going to be a viable alternative. I resolve not to take any more calls from either of the valley sisters. I go to sleep.

The next morning I fault myself for not having grabbed my video camera. It was a pretty amazing catfight.

GARDEN STATE INTERLUDE
PART II

Dad calls me from San Francisco. It's 4:00 pm on a Friday. He sounds agitated.

"Richard, I am in San Francisco. The Court of Appeals had an emergency conference in one of my cases and it is too late to get out of here and back to Newark."

"Why don't you fly down to LA and we can have lunch tomorrow. You can make the 3:00 pm."

"Fine," he says. I have the very distinct impression that the Court of Appeals is not seeing things as my father would like them to.

I take him to lunch in Westwood. It isn't so different from most other Saturdays. We go to L' Express.

Julie the hostess says "Hi, Richard."

I order an omelet. My father orders a club sandwich with turkey. I notice it has sprouts on it. It is the perfect opportunity to make an anti-California remark. He doesn't say anything. Something is clearly on his mind.

"Richard, you've been out here for a while now."

"Yes, Sir."

"Where are you going with this?"

"I'm not sure I understand what you mean when you say 'going with this.'"

"Richard, you don't surf. You don't produce movies. You don't represent celebrities. You just eat omelets served by waitresses with big tits who call you by your first name. You could do the same thing in New York."

I'm not sure what to say.

There is a lot of silence in the car on the way back to the airport.

When we get to the *Zona Blanca* for immediate loading and unloading only at the airport, I pop the trunk, pull out my father's bag and put it on the curb. I shake his hand and make direct eye contact.

"I really appreciate you sharing your concerns," I say.

Just when I get onto the 405, I start thinking that this California shit is really getting to me.

DIRTY DEBUTANT

The shirt lady is waiting in my office.

She is sitting in front of my desk. Of course she is the same office manager that had warned me that using my Dictaphone only to dictate letters is like using my microwave oven only to defrost ice cream.

I notice vaguely that the shirt lady's skirt is hiked up three quarters of the way up her thigh.

"Check the collar," says the shirt lady. I'm thinking that I should start calling her the skirt lady.

She studies me.

"Up all night?" says the shirt lady.

I smile.

"Thinking with the little head, not the big head?" says the shirt lady.

She peers at her tape measure.

"Still 15 1/2," she says. "$700 will get you ten."

"You're not getting cheaper," I say. At least she isn't telling me I am making an investment in my future like the dentist and the Mercedes salesman, I think.

"Nothing cheap about me." She pulls down her hiked up skirt.

"You got time for a drink?" I ask.

"It's 11:00 am, Richard. I don't drink before noon. If you still got the urge, you should get a refund for dinner from whomever you were banging last night. Guys get lucky and they think they can have their way with anybody."

As I reflect on this choice bit of female philosophy, the shirt lady once again pulls down her hiked up skirt and heads out the door. I turn to the papers on my desk. One of the MID LEVEL PARTNERS has decided that I should become a member of the firm's recruiting committee. The idea is to "integrate" me into the administration of the firm. I have been encouraged to seek out the key talents of young lawyers that would build the future of our firm: good grades, greed, and a desire to please at all costs. Of course, there are perks. I have basically an unlimited expense account for entertaining 22 year olds. I am soon known by every Maître D' of every decent French restaurant in Los Angeles.

I start wadding through the stacks of resumes from law students who want to work at this sweat shop. Probably better off working for the shirt lady at her factory in East Los Angeles.

The first resume is from a fellow from Ohio whose interest in the law would be better served by him becoming a policeman. The next resume in the stack gets my attention.

In fact, I am absolutely fascinated.

Samantha is clearly not in my target age range. So, she is older. There are some delicious little snippets in her resume: "1974 – Runway Model, Milan, Italy" and "1977-1978 – Agency for International Development, Geneva."

Samantha is a spy. Why she wanted to trade in cold war intrigue for a career consisting of ritualistic combat with Latin nouns is beyond me.

My Spy v. Spy Fantasy is immediately tempered by the fact that I have just become the junior member of the law school recruiting committee. You are clearly not supposed to be lusting after the recruits – other than as future profit centers.

I am interviewing Samantha a few days later in my office.

She is dressed very conservatively in a black suit. Black hair. She still has a model's legs. An absolute knock out.

"You have a real woman's resume," I say.

She laughs.

"I bet you drive a stick shift," I say.

"As a matter of fact, I do."

She had a great laugh.

"So, what can I tell you about the firm?" I try to sound sincere.

"I have a couple of good friends here from law school."

"Well, are you talking to anybody else?" The thought of Samantha working for another downtown law firm gives me an immediate hard on.

"Not really."

She starts two weeks later.

Three weeks later, she drops into my office. I look up from the tax code. Why did the corporate guys always want to use preferred stock? The IRS hates it and so do I.

"They are having a party for my birthday. Can you come?"

"Great."

Samantha lives in 1930 vintage apartment right where Beverly Hills becomes West Hollywood.

A very cute little French girl with big red lips and blond hair down to her butt answers the door.

"I'm Francine."

"I'm Richard. I work at that same law firm as Samantha."

"I'm just a shop girl," says Francine.

"It must be a very expensive shop."

"Very."

Samantha appears in a red leather mini wearing one blue shoe and one red shoe.

I look disapprovingly.

She hands me a glass of champagne.

"It's my birthday and I can wear anything I want. I don't want to match."

I agree. Samantha is more than a little tipsy and I am not going to pick a fight.

I eat cheese and water crackers and survey the crowd. Very cosmopolitan for LA. In addition to the normal Beverly Hills lineup of plastic surgeons, antiques dealers and scummy investment advisors, there are a few Italian and French executive types.

Samantha interrupts my conversation with the plastic surgeon and his nurse, who has clearly been the beneficiary of the latest breakthrough in enhancement technology.

"When are we going to have dinner?"

"Next Friday."

I take Samantha to the Ivy. Samantha turns out to be partial to miniskirts during nonworking hours. This one is accessorized by fishnets.

I nurse a vodka tonic and watch Samantha wolf down two dozen Kumamoto oysters. Then I watch as Samantha attacks a New York strip on the very rare side.

"I didn't think models ate like that."

"They don't. They are all anorexic. Strictly gum and apples."

"Uh-huh."

"This is so good. The meat in Europe stinks. That is why the French have five mother sauces."

"Uh-huh."

"And don't worry about fucking me. I am getting divorced."

"Are you sure you're not from California?"

Again the addictive laugh. I am thinking that Samantha's marital status is the least of my problems, unless her soon to be ex-husband is a gun collector. I am mentally reviewing exactly what THE MANAGING PARTNER is going to tell me when he finds out I have been using my office as a casting couch.

"Did you work for the CIA?"

Samantha smiles. She leans forward. I can see her breasts. She observes me observing her.

"You know I can't confirm or deny."

We walk on Rodeo. Samantha knows what she is doing. She runs to shop windows and gets two steps in front of me so I have a clear view of her ass. We end up petting in the doorway of Fendi.

The rest of the evening is a blur. I drift off to sleep remembering Samantha straddling me and murmuring "put it in my bottom."

IN THE BUBBLE

The next morning I wake up with the sudden realization that I am not in my condo in Westwood and that I am in the company of one of my fellow associates who is stark naked and serving me an espresso in a little white cup.

"How about a blow job?"

"Are you always this accommodating?"

"I'm a woman in love."

I roll into work at 11:00 am. I'm feeling drained. I am thinking that Freud is right. The mind is a hydraulic system. What exits from the penis cannot exit from the pen. Samantha has drained me of all of my creative energy.

That night I end up in Samantha's bed. I watch Miami Vice. Stylized violence in pastels. Samantha gives me another blow job.

I am feeling reflective.

"I need to get rich," I say.

Samantha gives me a knowing look.

"LA is no fun for the middle class," she says. "I will introduce you to my landlord. She knows the sacred nomenclature of real estate."

"What is that suppose to mean?" I ask.

"I'm not sure," Samantha says. "It is just something the Anthropology Professor would say at Sarah Lawrence. He was very insistent about it. He who controls the sacred nomenclature controls the symbolic environment."

"This guy must have owned a Volvo and screwed undergraduates," I say.

"He screwed a lot of his students," Samantha says. "Come to think of it, I think he did have a Volvo – a station wagon."

Beatrice is the widow of some guy who owned a chain of dry cleaners in the San Fernando Valley. I'm sure she killed him with too much brisket.

She looks a little frumpish, but evidences an iron will.

"I'm buying in Santa Barbara. You will come."

"Beatrice, I'm just a young lawyer."

"Good. You have cash flow."

I notice that Beatrice is driving an El Camino.

"Don't see too many of those in Beverly Hills," I say. In fact, I think, she is the first person of non-Hispanic origin that I have ever seen behind the wheel of that particular vehicle.

"Tax deduction," she says. "Utility Vehicle."

I am impressed. I decide to come along.

We drive to Santa Barbara. I see those same pink "This is bank of A. Levy Country" signs.

Beatrice talks in the car. Hubby was a serious drunk. After a while, he started sleeping with her friends. Beatrice made other friends, but got sick of picking him up off the floor in downtown bars where they only sell airline miniatures. She told him he was on his own. He committed suicide shortly thereafter.

"Richard, I can get you one on these for five percent down."

Beatrice is pointing to a 1950's tract home.

"Beatrice, the cash flow is negative."

"Richard, these homes are appreciating at twenty percent per annum. Put whatever discount rate you want on the negative cash flow. Samantha says you were smart."

Beatrice has gotten to me.

A week later I am in the office of the President of Universal Savings and Loan in Santa Monica

The President is an older gentleman, who is pretty clearly getting serviced by Beatrice. His lower lip sometimes twitches when Beatrice smiles at him.

"Any friend of Beatrice is a friend of mine." He smiles.

In a matter of six weeks I return to Santa Barbra four times. I am now the obligor on six different mortgages.

Two weeks later I have a drink with Beatrice at the bar at the Ivy in Beverly Hills.

"I did the calculations. My entire income is going to debt service."

"Exactly. If you need money, I will get you a second mortgage."

This only calms me down slightly. In the next few days I find the panic is slowly building. After all, I am a tax lawyer at a white shoe downtown law firm, not the dictator of a third world country. I have reached a level of fiscal irresponsibility equivalent to that of the government of Nigeria.

The panic subsides. Life has taken on a more predictable quality.

I work. I drink after work with the other associates. I drive home to Westwood. I change my clothes. I drive to Samantha's, take off my clothes, put on a sweat suit, give Samantha a spanking and fuck her ass. On Saturday, I drive to Santa Barbara with Beatrice and buy more houses that I have never actually been inside of.

On Saturday, I drive to Santa Barbara with Beatrice and buy more houses that I never actually been inside of. On Saturday, I sit by the swimming pool with Samantha who sunbathes topless, and pay tax bills to weed abatement districts and various mortgage companies. After two hours in the sun, Samantha gets very horny. We drive to Trashy Lingerie. Samantha presents her membership card and buys little teddies in various shades of purple, which leave her nipples and crotch exposed and we engage in more anal sex.

Next weekend we drive to Palm Desert. Samantha has friends with a house designed by Richard Nutria with a swimming pool. It has boulders in the living room. It is really hot. The outside temperature must be 105 degrees. With this kind of heat exposure, Samantha gets really horny and we have to go to the cabana more than once where she pulls down my bathing suit and busies herself with my bottom. Samantha seems to consider the day's challenge to reach my prostate gland with her tongue.

On the way back we stop at one of those dried fruit stands. I buy 200 feet of licorice and tell Samantha that we are going to do bondage.

I tie her up with strips of red licorice and she giggles and we have yet more anal sex. I congratulate myself on the innovative manipulation of the symbolic environment.

However, the comfort of routine soon gives way to more panic. I need a serious conversation with Beatrice. I make a date with Beatrice for next Saturday. I choose a coffee shop on Ventura Boulevard that I know from my days of obtaining releases from porno stars. I am very serious.

"Beatrice, I want to liquidate everything."

"You want to dump Samantha too?"

"Yes. I am going to do that too. But I still want to liquidate everything."

I sign a lot of papers and when it is all over I have $450,000 and change in my market rate account at Universal Savings.

Beatrice wants to introduce me to a friend in Newport Beach who sells Kugerrands for investment, but I drag my feet.

I have already dodged one bullet. I am starting to think the agent Orange crazed Mercenaries were just child's pay. The problem with LA is that the real killers drive nice cars and wear Rolex watches with diamond bezels.

I am increasingly conflicted about Samantha. The notion that I could be bored by a steady diet of anal sex with a former spy is not registering. I feel that something must be wrong with me.

I drive down to Newport Beach with her to meet Blitstein. He is interviewing for jobs.

Samantha is going through this California assimilation thing and spends the whole trip with her head on my lap sucking on my penis. After a few erratic lane changes I finally come on the 133 right after I turn off of the 405. The windshield is so steamed up that I have to stop for a few minutes on Forrest and crack open the window before I turn onto Third. Samantha is still busy in my lap.

Blitstein is not impressed with Samantha. We have a brief moment when Samantha is in the bathroom.

"You think she's hot, because she's a debutante," he says.

I am peeved.

"That almost rhymes," I say.

However, the inevitable process of disengagement has begun.

Samantha and I stop at the Cosmic Age Motor Inn outside of Santa Anna, which is somewhere that I always wanted to have sex. For the first time with Samantha, something is missing.

The firm announces shortly thereafter that it is opening an office in Washington, D.C. Samantha decides that she misses all of her friends in the agency that she still refuses to identify.

A tearful, at least a few, farewell.

I still think fondly of that one stretch of the 405.

ESCAPE

Word in the pub is that the MIDLEVEL PARTNER has been impressing senior management. In other words, his clients have been spending even more than the usual obscene amounts of money on legal fees. They are going to make him responsible for opening the firm's office in New York.

My calendar says that it is September. I am summoned to a corner office.

The MIDLEVEL PARTNER has his jacket on and his desk is clear except for one file.

It is pretty clearly my file.

"Richard, you have accomplished quite a bit here in Los Angeles."

"Thank you, sir."

I am thinking that something geographic is going on. Why mention Los Angeles? You can see the Santa Monica freeway over his left shoulder.

"Uh. Hum. Shown some real range here. I see here that in addition to your fine tax work that you are quite the entertainment lawyer."

"Thank you, sir." I am thinking of Ms. Moan's unmovable breasts.

"I'd like to invite you to become part of our Manhattan project. I want you right behind me when we take on the biggest firms in the United States."

I pause. The realization hits me that the MIDLEVEL PARTNER is a complete moron. He doesn't seem to realize that the Manhattan project was Franklin Roosevelt's secret mission to develop the atomic bomb and that it was located in the desert sands of New Mexico. I

159

guess they don't teach that stuff at land grant colleges. The MIDLEVEL PARTNER also doesn't have a clue that he sounds like a like a dam sodomite with the "I want you right behind me" routine.

I make direct eye contact. I have lived in LA long enough to control the symbolic environment.

I am trying to appear reflective and deliberate, but my thoughts are racing. Had I been in LA too long? The intersection of the 405 and 10 freeway had already been a point of climax with no fewer than four different women. Was change in order? Should I be doing afternooners in that sleazy looking hotel on 47th and Lexington?

"Richard, this would be a great career move for you."

I translate instantly. The threat is clear. My career will suffer if I forsake the big apple for the big orange. Time is frozen. The breathing of the MIDLEVEL PARTNER becomes deliberate and labored. I pause to think.

I suddenly feel flushed with new resolve. LA doesn't even have a downtown. Where am I going with this LA thing? My parents will greet the news of my return to New York like my acceptance to Harvard Law School. I remember my father's parting words. There is plenty of sex in New York.

"I'm right behind you, sir," I say.

The MIDLEVEL PARTNER gives me a toothy LA smile.

I am humming "those East Coast girls are hip I hear."

However, that is another story.